CROSSING THE BAR

The story of Daniel Opong Amoafo (DO)
(An Educationist)

Kofi Otutu Adu Labi

Other Books by the Author
Pearls of Wisdom
Nuggets for Victorious Living
Stories to Warm your Heart
Wisdom, Faith and a Song
They Touched us for Good
From Subri Anafoɔ to Pepease and Dansoman
All Things Bright and Beautiful
Musings from the HillTop

Copyright @ 2020, Kofi Otutu Adu Labi

ISBN: 978-9988-9029-7-1

Published by Digibooks Ghana Ltd.
P. O. Box BT1, Tema, Ghana
Tel: +233-303-414-720 / +233-246-493-842
Email: admin@digibookspublishing.com
Website: http://www.digibookspublishing.com

DEDICATION

To Daniel Opong Amoafo (DO) and all the
nonagenarians out there who have been good enough
to share their stories so that those coming after them
will learn from their achievements as well as their
challenges.

TABLE OF CONTENTS

FOREWORD

The American author and New York Times bestseller S.E. Hall puts it like this: Maybe it is not the length of time you have known someone; maybe it is about instant recognition at an unconscious level. Our souls know each other. To put it another way, connections make the world go round.

I have never met the man for whose biography I am privileged to write this foreword. And yet I have met him. And that is the mystery of our existential connections. When my friend and brother Mr. Kofi Otutu Adu Labi, who is the author of this book requested that I write a foreword for it, he added that the person whose biography it is happens to be the father of my friend and former student Cynthia Amoafo.

I think Kofi added that connection to spice up my interest. I am sure I would not dream of refusing any request by the author who has dedicated his life to writing about the noble side of life. He goes out of his way to bring to us the best in our people through his books which inform, educate and motivate thousands of people every day.

But adding the Cynthia spice worked too. She was a brilliant student when I taught her class English and English literature for their O Levels at Aburi Girls' Secondary School in the 1970s. Later, as a friend of friends at University, I kept in touch with her. She has excelled at her career in Ghana's Civil Service and risen to the top of that slippery career poll. She is a disciplined person and yet has such splendid sense of humour. The connection was made. I wanted to read about her father. Then, even more connections: I discovered that Mr. D. O. Amoafo, whose biography it is was a teacher at Apam Secondary School where I did my 6th Form. I think he must have left the year I went there. He was thus my nearly-teacher, as I describe such close encounters that never were.

I have to thank Kofi for the privilege he has given me not only to contribute to this book but more importantly, to know Mr. Amoafo. It is a splendid idea to write this book to celebrate this brilliant and unpretentious Ghanaian who through his own hard work and dedication to his ideals achieved so much for his country, his family and himself. It is the story of a man who has been described rightly as an educationist. For him, service to his country was and remains his highest creed after service to God.

The life of the person the reader will encounter in this book has been defined by two words often joined in a cliché, for God and country. On this occasion, those two entities – God and country – are the two pillars on which Mr. Amoafo hung his fate and faith. Then, there was his commitment to family. Family meant both nuclear and extended; there was no real distinction because the ties that bound them together were not defined by the precise relationships but by the energy that flowed within the common spaces even when they were not physically together.

This book is about one patriot but in a way, it is also a book about a generation to which our country needs to pay a huge debt of gratitude. This is why although I have never met Mr. Amoafo in the flesh, I do recognize him on every page in the book. His generation was the first to accept the challenges of local leadership after independence. They were the cadres who actualized the challenge of decolonizing the civil service, education, health, local government and the security services. They accepted postings to places that lacked water and electricity without a murmur. They were pioneers in all fields of endeavor and true heroes of development.

This book, which is the story of one man, is effectively a social history of Ghana in microcosm expertly captured by the biographer. The book will be useful beyond its immediate purpose of telling Mr. Amoafo's life story. It will explain to many young readers the foundations of our country as they were laid by the men and women who came of age at the time people of their calibre were required. For me, it has been a huge privilege to get to know this man through the pages of this book.

Nana Kwasi Gyan-Apenteng
Former Chairman, National Media Commission.
Consultant in media, culture and communication.
Immediate past President, Ghana Association of Writers.

ACKNOWLEDGMENTS

I have known Daniel Opong Amoafo for about 35 years, but I never, in my wildest imagination, thought that I would write a book about him at some point in the future.

That this improbability has become a possibility is solely due to the determination of Cynthia Asare Bediako, his daughter and distinguished civil servant, to have the life of her father chronicled for posterity.

In the process, it has been a fascinating literary journey for me. I am grateful to Cynthia for supplying me with the basic raw material which I used to build what has evolved, to all intents and purposes, into a very readable, enjoyable and educative life story.

I am also grateful to Dada Amoafo, as I call him, for his friendship over the years which helped me in no small way to put different strands together in writing this biography.

His youngest brother, Lawrence Benjamin Amoafo provided useful background information for which I am grateful.

Ohui Agbenyega Allotey, renowned Editor and avid reader, used her experience to offer very useful suggestions and pointed out areas needing adjustment.

My friends Seth Osafo and Josephine Osafo-Affum also took the trouble to read over the manuscript and provided very useful comments. My children Abena Okyerebea and Kofi Otutu Jnr as usual gave a lot of backroom support to the project.

Finally, I appreciate the immense support from Fred Labi and his team at Digibooks for the invaluable feedback and support they gave me.

ENDORSEMENTS

"Young people today want to get things fast but there are no shortcuts in life. Success is achieved one step at a time and by being diligent in the small things before the big things come our way. This book about the life of DO Amoafo reveals a lot of principles that can guide us along life's journey. You will enjoy it".

Rev. Prof. Mrs. Ivy Drafor Amenyah
Director, Research, Innovation & Consultancy Centre, Pentecost University
MBTI Certified Leadership Training Consultant, Agenda Inspirations
Ordained Minister, Presbyterian Church of Ghana

• • •

I have read many voluminous biographies, and was thus apprehensive of what this book might hold within its (153) pages. I am pleasantly surprised at the poignant lessons in life skills, reminders of our cultural practices and their roots, as well as valuable historical accounts of the past of our dear country all packaged into this short biography. DO, the subject, has lived through the changing scenes of life, portraying the often hidden turbulence, confusion, fears and flights of emotions encountered throughout the growing up process.

This biography is a lesson in the heights attainable through humility, discipline, perseverance, and faith in God; epitomizing the adage *"Obi nnim Obrempong n'ahyease"*. A lesson from the OLD is GOLD.

A must read for both the young and old.

Edusei Derkyi
Banker, Author and
Member, Ghana Association of Writers (GAW) Advisory Board

• • •

"Crossing the Bar", the ninth book by the distinguished author Kofi Adu Labi, is a very rewarding and exciting literary piece. This book which recounts the life of Mr. D.O. Amoafo of Abetifi and Nkwatia-Kwahu, has done justice to a great man's life. It is Mr. Adu Labi's second book which recounts the life of a remarkable nonagenarian. Like the first one which was about Mr. Eugene Ernest Amoa, there are several important lessons to be learned. This book which should be a welcome addition to anybody who is interested in Ghana's traditions and historical transition from the World War II period through colonial times and post-independence to the present day. A major lesson a reader will come away with is that one's journey in life will be shaped by whatever you do with the opportunities that come your way, your attitude to life and God's grace and mercies.

The book will take the reader through the life of an educationist, businessman, historian, lay preacher and a family man. From his auspicious birth in Bechem in 1930 through to his secondary school life at Presbyterian Secondary School in Odumase Krobo, then to the

Presbyterian Training College and eventually to the University of Ghana, the story is vividly told. The picture of an industrious and enterprising young man, with business acumen and a sense of community, emerges easily for the reader. His experiences as a Boy Scout leader, pupil teacher and then a trained teacher honed his leadership skills. His contribution to nurturing the Dansoman Emmanuel Congregation of the Presbyterian Church of Ghana (PCG) from its formative years is also recounted. In all of this, one will gain insights into the life and practices of a responsible family man: the interesting account of his marriage to his dear Margaret; and the successful children that emerged from that partnership as fruits of effective parenting. Yet the reader also realizes that the life of a successful man is not all a bed of roses; Mr. Amoafo's disappointments and bereavements are also shared. The book includes tributes from family and former students, all pointing to a well-rounded patriarch. It is telling that it concludes with ten lessons for effective living which include persistence, hard work and genuine love.

"Crossing the Bar" is certainly a "must-have" in every discerning person's library.

Esther Oduraa Ofei-Aboagye (PhD)
Chair, STAR Ghana Foundation and
Development Management Consultant

Writing with the skill of an accomplished author of eight previous books, Kofi Otutu Adu Labi's ninth book delightfully chronicles the life history of 90 year old D.O. Amoafo in this easy to read book.

The author's description of the ups and downs of DO's life showing his rise from a potential illiterate farmer which his father wanted him to be, to a famous academic, emphasises the importance of perseverance, determination and above all trusting in God in all we do.

I highly recommend this book to all.

Brig. General Dan Frimpong (Rtd)

Former CEO, African Peace Support Trainers Association (APSTA)
Nairobi, Kenya
Council Chairman, Family Health University College,
Teshie, Accra, Ghana

• • •

This has been a captivating read from beginning to end. I had intended reading it at a leisurely pace but soon realised it was 'unputdownable', from the moment I started. My attention was caught right from the start by names which brought back memories:

- My mother was also born in Bechem in 1940 (10 years after DO) where my grandfather, a Presbyterian minister, was then stationed.

- My earliest memory (possibly age 2) of my own life, is of Abetifi where, again, my grandfather was stationed at the time.

- Mention of 'Pomaa' rather than 'ponewa' (which is the female derivative of 'Opong' used in my family).

I am delighted to have been among the first to read this inspirational biography of, by all accounts, an inspirational man.

You will be enriched by reading it and I recommend that you get a copy immediately.

Elizabeth Frimpomah Arhin
HR Consultant

• • •

CROSSING THE BAR, the story of Daniel Opong Amoafo (DO), an Educationist is captivating, inspirational and makes an interesting reading piece.

The chronology and clarity of the narrative attests to the author's love for history and strong personal relationships. These he has skilfully encapsulated to espouse the life and intrinsic worth of DO.

DO epitomises the virtues of hard work, perseverance, discipline and being results-oriented.

Indeed, he lived by the words of the Good Book in Colossians 3:23 that *"Whatever you do, work at it with all your heart, as working for the Lord, not for human masters."*

This is a must read book. Get a copy.

Robert Dwamena
Fellow and Past President, Ghana Institution of Surveyors
Former Managing Director, Electricity Company of Ghana (ECG)

DO has been a brother to me since 1948 when I came to live with his aunt Akosua Biraa to study at the Abetifi Girls School. My parents were peasant farmers in the Afram Plains. I was readily accepted by DO and his cousins, but he singled me out and showed me extra love and care.

I have always known him to have a big heart. He is very peaceful and loved by family and friends for this warm character.

I was privileged to witness his wedding in 1966 after he had witnessed mine a year before.

DO's life is an illustration of the adage that while there is life there is hope. I encourage readers of this fascinating account of DO's life to learn of him, with special reference to responsible parenting, prayerfulness and the fear of God.

I have thoroughly enjoyed reading this book. I wish you happy reading too.

Alice Adarkwa Dadzie
(Afua Asaa)
Retired Educationist

INTRODUCTION

This biography of Daniel Opong Amoafo (DO) has been written by me as a result of the passion of his daughter Cynthia Asare Bediako, a Chief Director in the Ghana Civil Service. Cynthia has, for a long time, been keen to have the life and experiences of her father (as told her by her father) chronicled for posterity. After she first approached me and we followed up with more conversations and exchanges, I fell in love with the project and accepted her request that I undertake the exercise. I have enjoyed this literary and historical journey and I am pleased that it has become a reality.

Life is a journey which everyone goes through. Between the time you are born and the day of your death, you go through various stages and seasons. What you become in life depends on what you do with the opportunities and obstacles that may come your way, the attitude you adopt and the grace and mercy of God. There could be other factors, but these are the principal ones that emerge out of the story of Daniel Opong Amoafo (DO) as narrated in this book.

Life is a race that must be run. There is no escaping from the call to race. How does one run in such a way as to win and leave imprints in the sands of time for others to follow? How does one respond to the sometimes overwhelming challenges that confront one at almost every stage?

Daniel Opong Amoafo (DO), in looking at the prism of his life after a full ninety (90) years, likens himself to an athlete in a high jump competition. I would add the pole vault as well. You can certainly picture the athlete attempting to clear the height or bar set as a starting minimum in the high jump or pole vault event. Invariably, the bars are set at levels higher than the previous best jumps of the athlete. The challenge is to see if the athlete will be motivated and determined enough to muster all his or her energies and will power to conquer, as it were, the new level or bar.

The bar is never set at a level that is easy or comfortable to jump or leap over. Indeed the bar can be intimidating and those without strong will-power and sense of determination may end up not being able to cross them, however naturally gifted they might be. The one who is able to clear the bar, ends up falling on the padded canvas with a sense of satisfaction and achievement. More often than not, there are a number of unsuccessful attempts before a clearance comes. The cheers from the spectators present make all the pain worthwhile. Things do not end there, however. New levels are then set and the competition continues till a champion emerges.

This book chronicles the life of DO, as he is referred to by friends and shares in some intriguing details from his early life to adulthood. There are lessons to be gleaned from what he has seen and experienced. He counsels young people to strive to work hard. He cautions against procrastination and advises that everyone should put their God-given talents to good use while it is day. Whatever happens, never give up.

"*Ade kyee, yɛfrɛ no ɔkyena*," was one of the things Mr. D. O. Amoafo told me soon after we had settled down for my extended interview with him.

Tomorrow does not belong to you, is an interpretation, not a literal translation of the Akan phrase above.

In a world full of uncertainty, there is a lot of wisdom in the above statement, which Mr. D. O. Amoafo is fond of. It is an admonition to all and sundry, especially the young, to beware of procrastination. Procrastination is a thief. He is a firm believer in the adage that whatever needs to be done ought to be done while there is an opportunity, instead of waiting for so-called perfect conditions. Do what you can today. A stitch in time saves nine. How sad it is to see and hear so many people with brilliant ideas and plans not settling down to the task immediately, while it is today. Time and tide wait for no man. The more you keep putting off what you can do today to tomorrow, the more likely it is that you may never get round to doing it. You will just end up building castles in the air. At the same time, it is good advice to us not to boast about tomorrow and make plans as if we were the determinants of time. Tomorrow does not belong to you.

Well has it been said that the most valuable piece of real estate is the cemetery. The land that contains all the rich ideas that never saw the light of day, all because of procrastination. As the Bible says, *'If you wait until the wind and the weather are just right, you will never plant anything and never harvest anything.'* Ecclesiastes 11:4 Good News Translation.

Proverbs 27:1 also says, *"do not boast about tomorrow, for you do not know what a day may bring."*

I had been looking forward to meeting Mr. D. O. Amoafo in March this year (2020). Some business had taken me out of Accra when he celebrated his 90th birthday, which fell on January 6, 2020. This was significant, as it fell on his day of birth, a Monday. The actual celebrations took place the following day, January 7, for good reason. With January 7 now a national holiday (Constitution Day), the holding of the landmark celebration on that date made it possible for many more loved ones to be present. From all accounts, it was a glorious celebration. My wife Elioenai represented me and joined family and friends from Ghana and abroad to celebrate a remarkable personality known for his wisdom, sense of history and wit. I had sent him a message that I would surely pay him a visit at home to extend my personal congratulations and also to have an interaction with him. I chose a Saturday that did not have any of the social demands on my time and set out for his Achimota residence. I had assumed, wrongly, that the traffic would be heavy so it was a pleasant surprise for me to get there in record time. It was as if all the elements were happy with the mission I was on and collaborated to ease the heavy traffic associated with that part of Accra for my sake.

What a warm smile he gave me as he stretched out his hand to me on entering his sitting room at Achimota, where I had arrived a few minutes earlier. The delight was mutual. This is someone I have known at church at Dansoman since early 1977 when I first joined the Presbyterian Church of Ghana, Emmanuel Congregation, Dansoman.

DO (third from left) with some friends at Dansoman Emmanuel Congregation of the Presbyterian Church.

His daughter Cynthia Asare Bediako, a distinguished civil servant, was present with another daughter, MyraStella Ansah at the time of my visit.

Mr. D. O. Amoafo, teacher, educationist, historian, preacher, businessman and a family icon of Abetifi Kwahu in the part of Ghana I call *'bepɔw a ɛtɔ so abien* (the second hill top) was known as a very convivial nature as an Elder at Dansoman Emmanuel Presbyterian Church in his earlier years. His sermons were always spiced with historical references topped with humorous applications one could not easily forget. Sometimes he would narrate a story and its application and just when you thought the sermon was over, he would announce that he was about to start. That would invariably bring the house down. Beyond that style was always something to learn about the recommended lifestyle of the Christian based on biblical values.

How can I also forget an incident that took place while Mr. E. E. Amoa, whose story I have told in my book, *From Subri Anafoɔ to Pepease and Dansoman*, was preaching one Sunday morning. Teacher Amoa, as he is affectionately referred to by many, asked DO, in the course of the sermon, to read a portion of Scripture to support a point he had made before continuing with his sermon. Teacher Amoa asked that only some particular verses be read and that the congregation should read the rest of the passage for the day at their leisure at home later in the day. DO went ahead to read the recommended passages but did not stop there. He paused and told Teacher

Amoa in words to this effect, "Kwaku, please, if you do not mind allow me to read the whole passage. You and I know our people and you can be sure that they will not undertake the reading exercise you are forcing down their throats when they get home." DO then proceeded to read the whole passage in flawless Asante Twi. This was part of his style. This was a teacher! A chip off the old block indeed.

I invite you to come along with me as we explore various segments of the life of Daniel (DO) Opong Amoafo.

Experience is the best teacher, and we shall all do well to learn from the lives of pacesetters so that we do not reinvent the wheel.

(Left to right) Mrs. Mary Opoku-Agyemang, DO and Madam Beatrice Lartey after church at Dansoman.

CHAPTER 1

The Beginnings

Daniel Opong Amoafo (DO) was born at Bechem at 12:30 in the afternoon, on January 6, 1930. That sounds very exact, especially for the place and period in time of his birth. The reason will be apparent soon. His parents were Opanyin Kwaku Amoafo of Nkwatia and Awo Akua Dwiraa of Abetifi, both in the Kwahu East District of the Eastern Region of Ghana. He was the sixth of fifteen children. His delivery was safe and without complications. He was born into the Asona Clan whose totem (*akraboa*) is the crow (*kwaakwaadabi*). The 'midwife' who delivered him was called Maame Abena Kwabena. Maame Abena Kwabena was an experienced traditional birth attendant in the area. She was famous for her predictions before and after delivery. For her accuracy, she was branded a witch by the younger generation.

Mr Amoafo (DO) believes he had two advantages over his siblings. His father, Opanyin Kwaku Amoafo, had gone to Bechem as a farmer and a cocoa agent to U.A.C (now known as Unilever). The father had a clerk/assistant who recorded the birth. This was not the case with the births of most of his siblings. The other advantage was being delivered by Maame Abena Kwabena, who had a reputation to prophesy and pronounce blessings over the babies she delivered. This celebrated birth attendant spoke into the future of the baby boy. He would grow up to become very useful in society and would influence many lives. Maame Abena Kwabena had also predicted that he would live to be older than most of his elder siblings. He would also be the duplicate of his father's uncle. It was this uncle who brought up his father. Further, he would grow up to share a lot in common with his elder brother J.A. Amoafo.

His mother kept these things in her heart (as Mary the mother of the baby Jesus did) and was very careful in his upbringing and nurturing.

As it turned out, all these predictions turned out to be true. You will discover, as you read along, that he became a prosperous businessman, a dedicated and influential teacher and a much respected figure in Church and Society.

CHAPTER 2

Family History

Daniel Opong Amoafo cherishes his family pedigree. I therefore deem it important to give some detail about his family history at the onset.

DO belongs to the Asona family of Abetifi and Nkwatia Kwahu. The Kwahus of Ghana are Akan. Like other Akan groups, the Kwahus are matrilineal, which means that the child is related to the mother by blood and thus belongs to the mother's family. The relationship to the father is by spirit. The child therefore belongs to the clan of the mother and that is how one's lineage is traced and in the Akan family lineage and context one's clan is determined by one's mother's lineage. Pay attention to what DO has to say about his clan. DO belongs to the Asona family of Abetifi and Nkwatia Kwahu. It is generally believed that the Asonas are handsome and beautiful people. *"Asona ni atiko te sɛ obi anim"* is a saying in Twi which loosely translates that the back of the Asona person's head is as beautiful as his face! The Asonas are also believed to be very intelligent. *"Asona ni ba a onnim nyansa no, na ne maame kɔɔ ntwakyea"* is said of them to the effect that it is only the child of a wayward Asona woman who does not have brains.

It is pertinent to note that most Ghanaians lay claim to having migrated from somewhere before finally settling at their present locations. Some Ga people, for example, believe that they migrated to Ghana from Israel. They insist that they are a lost tribe of Israel. That is not a subject for discussion in this book though. So, it is with DO Amoafo's family.

According to DO, his great grandmother was called Aberewa Afua Nyarkoa. She was popularly referred to as Ofusii during her lifetime. This was a name given to her by her neighbours due to her inability to communicate with them in the Twi language after she and her sister first arrived in Abetifi. Ofusii was a corrupted form of *"Onfusi wo"* loosely translated as "the one who will not respond when spoken to." Over time this became the name by which the townsfolk referred to her, even long after she was able to communicate fluently in Twi.

This great woman was an Ewe and believed to be a member of the Akpini Royal family of Kpando in the Volta Region of Ghana. It is said that during an inter tribal war in the late 1800s, she and her younger sister by name Nana Yaa (otherwise known as Onuapa) were taken captive by two young Kwahu warriors. These young warriors, Kofi Kodua and Kwame Okyere, ferried the two sisters over the Oti river and brought them down to Nkwatia to settle in the Chief's palace. Afua

4

Nyarkoa was quite matured and said to be pregnant at the time of her capture. She delivered a still-born baby while trekking with her captors. The royals of Nkwatia were (and are) of the Asona clan and so they got the clan elders to assimilate these young ladies into the clan. The young Afua Nyarkoa and her sister Nana Yaa were said to be beautiful and hard working girls. The chief of Nkwatia took notice of them and told his Elders that these gems of young women should marry from within the royal family. He was convinced that they would bring forth offspring who would grow to become a blessing to Nkwatia and beyond. Afua Nyarkoa and Nana Yaa were therefore settled a short distance from Nkwatia, precisely at Abetifi with the Asona clan there to continue the linkage with the Nkwatia side of the Asona clan. The strategic thinking behind this move was to make any future marriage between any Nkwatia men and Afua Nyarkoa and her sister appear normal, so to speak. Needless to say, one of the men from the Asona clan of Nkwatia, by name Kofi Kodua, married the young Afua Nyarkoa. They had two children, namely, Akua Biraa and Abena Odurowaa. Kofi Kodua died not long after the birth of the second daughter Abena Odurowaa and in line with the customary practice of the day, his brother Kwame Okyere married his widow Afua Nyarkoa. You will recall the two young warriors who captured the young Afua Nyarkoa and her sister in war. These two, Kofi Kodua and Kwame Okyere, are indeed the ones who married Afua Nyarkoa in turn.

The union produced one child, Adwoa Boaduwaa. The arranged marriage yielded good results. Each of these three also got married and had their line of children. DO's line is traced from Abenaa Oduruaa; who gave birth to nine children, including a set of twins as follows: Kwaku Anim, Kwame Anim, Akua Dwiraa, Akua Dankwaa, Kwaku Osei, Abenaa Dentaa, Ata Panyin, Ata Kuma, Yaa Asabea Tawia. In effect, Afua Nyarkoa's clan, which could be the definitive determination of the real clan of DO and his siblings, by Akan custom, can only be settled when the lineage to Kpando is re-established. Suffice it to say for now that they have so far been effectively infused into the Asona clan of Abetifi.

DO's Mother

Awo Akua Dwiraa was the mother of DO Amoafo. She died in 1978 at the age of 78. She was the 3rd born of Awo Abenaa Odurowa who happened to be the second born of the union between Abrewa Afua Nyarkoa and Opanyin Kofi Kodua. Awo Dwiraa's father was called Opanyin Yaw Obiri and was by extension DO's grandfather.

Awo Akua Dwiraa, DO's mother, married her life time husband Opanyin Kwaku Amoafo at a very young age. Indeed, it is believed that Opanyin Kwaku Amoafo got Akua Dwiraa (DO's mother) betrothed to him when she was in her mother's womb (very young). In the Akan tradition this is known as *"Asiwa."* It is said that Opanyin Kwaku Amoafo provided for the care of the young Akua Dwiraa right from the womb, and even built a house for DO's grandmother, Nana Odurowaa, before the marriage was formalised. The house still stands at Abetifi, bearing witness to this family history.

Since she was betrothed at a very tender age, her husband was well advanced in years and already an experienced family man. Opanyin Kwaku Amoafo already had a wife known as Maame Yaa Bosuo and five children before Akua Dwiraa was brought into the relationship. These children were Abena Oforiwaa, Yaa Anyanewaa Panyin, Kwasi Amoafo, Abena Animwaa and Kwabena Oduro (Paul Oduro Amoafo).

Not long after Akua Dwiraa came into the scene, as a young bride, the first marriage of his father collapsed. Paul who was at that time just about three (3) years old stayed with Awo Dwiraa. As a young wife Awo Akua Dwiraa was very fertile. She also had a lot of hands to help her in her household chores and other family responsibilities due to the presence of the other older children from the first marriage. She therefore literally concentrated her efforts to expanding the Amoafo family.

The union was blessed and her dream fulfilled. DO's mother gave birth to fifteen (15) children, ten (10) of whom lived up to advanced ages. The 10 children of Akua Dwiraa who lived to old age (and indeed a few are still alive) are, Kwadwo Osei, Kwabena Aning "Donkor" (JA), Afua Agyeiwaa, Kwadwo Opong (Kwadwo Kuma or DO), Yaa Nyarkoa, Yaa Anyanewaa, Yaw Adofo, Kwadwo Badu (Nyantakyi), Abenaa Duku (Asantewaa) and Ama Adusa (Biraa).

It was the wish of their elders to have the Nyarkoa pedigree implanted in the family. To this end, Opanyin Kwaku Amoafo's only brother by name Yaw Obimpeh (also known as Twenefuor Boama) married Akua Dwiraa's cousin from Awo Biraa's line by name Napanyin Akosua Asantewaa. They had four children. The two brothers therefore married from the same house and this has in a sense contributed to the strong bonds existing within the Amoafo clan. This story is recounted here to establish the very close link between DO's family and their ancestors in Kpando in the Volta Region. What a lovely story line; from Abrewa Nyarkoa (Ofusii) to Eno Odurowaa to Awo Dwiraa and to DO. The story is sure to continue and given the ways of the world a member of the family from the other side (Kpando) will surely read this book and lead a delegation to Kwahu for a reunion. What a day that will be!

The little research for this book has led to the tracing of the Amoafo Family Tree and it has created a lot of excitement and desire to reconnect with the Kpando relations.

The Family Tree is shown as Appendix 3.

DO's Dad – Opanyin Kwaku Amoafo

DO's Mum – Awo Dwiraa

CHAPTER 3

Elder Brother James Kwabena Aning Amoafo and the Origins of Opong

The story of James Kwabena Aning Amoafo is recounted here for two reasons.

First, and as indicated in Chapter 1, Maame Abena Kwabena, the traditional birth attendant who delivered DO had said that he would take after his elder brother J. A. Amoafo. Second, these two brothers grew up to share a lot in common and stood out, professionally, among their siblings in their adult lives.

At the time Maame Abena Kwabena spoke, no one could imagine the way and manner in which what she said would unravel, but as fate would have it, these two brothers grew up to look physically alike. They also became the icons and gems of the family in every sense, through the heights they reached and the positive influence they brought to bear on many lives, within and outside their immediate families.

According to DO, JA became his role model and as an elder brother, it was not difficult for him to follow the footsteps of JA.

At this juncture, it will be appropriate to provide a little background information on this role model of DO. James Amoafo (JA) was born on a Tuesday and therefore called Kwabena, the name given to every Tuesday born Akan male. His full name was James Kwabena Aning Amoafo. However, because two siblings preceding him died and in order to ward off evil spirits attacking him and killing too as a baby (in accordance with the Akan belief system), tribal marks were put on his face, ostensibly to make him unattractive to them.

He was also given another name, Donkor, to give the impression to the spirits believed to be lurking around that he was alien to the family, indeed a slave, whose soul was not worth attacking. This belief was prevalent at the time. To his immediate family and friends though, he was affectionately called and known as JA.

His primary school education took place at the Bechem Presbyterian Primary and Middle Schools from 1932 to 1942. He was a brilliant pupil and student with a wonderful aptitude in the English language. He was in the third batch of pupils to sit the Standard 7 examinations at the Bechem Presbyterian Middle School. He passed with Distinction, having topped his class all the way from Class 1 to Standard 7. From Primary and Middle school he went on to pursue his post-secondary education at the Presbyterian Secondary School (Presec) at Krobo Odumase where he earned Distinction in the Cambridge School Certificate examinations. He then went on to do his sixth form at the St. Augustine's

College, Cape Coast and after two academic terms there he earned Grade One with Exemption in the then Cambridge University entrance examinations. He then went on to the Presbyterian Training College, Akropong Akuapem, where he was trained as a Teacher/Catechist. He proceeded to the University College of the Gold Coast (now University of Ghana), being in the second batch of students to enter the University, which was then at Achimota. In 1955, he earned a Bachelor's Degree in Sociology and Economics.

JA was the "first gentleman" of the family. Interestingly, their father, Opanyin Kwaku Amoafo, was in the habit of making excuses for not sending his children to school when they reached school going age. He had a fascination for his farms and always wished to have his sons with him on the farm or close by him. One of his cherished ambitions when he was young was to name a son after a loved uncle or relation. After some initial round of excuses, he allowed JA to go to school and he did not disappoint. That is how come JA became the "first gentleman" of the family.

J. A. Amoafo, who died on February 24, 2013 at the age of 87, had a a long and distinguished working life which took him to Abuakwa State College (as Assistant Headmaster), Ghana Secondary School, Koforidua, the Ghana Academy of Arts and Sciences, the Council for Scientific and Industrial Research, the Institute of African Studies and the Ghana Institute of Languages.

J.A Amoafo (DO's Brother)

Origin of the Name Opong

DO's name 'Opong' was that of his father's uncle and a much loved uncle for that matter. However, when he was a child, DO hated to be called 'Opong' as his uncles used to tease him with it. He hated it because they had the tendency to call the Kwadwo and Opong together in the traditional way, KoOpong, and this had a funny twist to it. But when he entered training college, something interesting happened which changed his world view about his name and he became happy, and indeed, excited to use it.

What could this development be? In the course of a Twi language class, one of his tutors at the Presbyterian Training College, Akropong, asked him if he knew the meaning of his name. He did not know, and as a matter of fact this question disoriented him. No one had ever asked him this question before and he had no clue as to what his name meant. The tutor then went ahead to explain the meaning of his name "Opong" to him as the rest of the class listened with rapt attention.

The tutor told him that "Opong' has the root of 'pon' which means the biggest or the grandest. Examples are *Akro-pon, (kurow kɛse), Onyanko-pɔn (Onyame baako-kɛse), Odu-pon (dua kɛse).*

This was an epiphany moment for the young DO. He started to reflect on his life and came to the realisation that he was not an ordinary person. He was 'Opong' and that there was something special about him. He was the

14

real McCoy, as the Americans will say and he was now happy to use his name, Opong. The rest, as the saying goes, is history.

He has, in his old age, fashioned out a common yell with his grandchildren and all those named after him as 'Opong.' The yell is "Okye-kyee" and the response is 'The Kuus"!!! The male grandchildren are called Opong while the females are known as Pomaa. Some families use 'Ponewaa' to denote female Opongs but he has always insisted that they should be called Pomaa. He is very proud of his grandchildren and all those named after him. He describes them as strong, intelligent and skilful.

He also loved to be called DO which sounded right in his ears, and still does today. Many of his friends call him simply as DO, but his town folks call him 'Teacher Amoafo'.

CHAPTER 4

Early Years

Sɛ wo te faako a, wo te wadeɛ so.

In other words, human life is not static. It is most unhelpful to remain at one stage of growth forever. You cannot realise your full potential if you just stay put. D.O. Amoafo seems to have inherited this belief from his parents, Opanyin Kwaku Amoafo of Nkwatia and Awo Akua Dwiraa of Abetifi, both towns in the Kwahu East District of the Eastern Region of Ghana.

Growing up, DO and his siblings were very much attached to Bechem, where their parents had settled for farming activities in Kwasuogya, a nearby farming community. They had their primary school education in Bechem and spent a lot of the school holidays in Bechem and on their father's farms at Kwasuogya. The whole family made annual "homecoming" trips to Kwahu. Those were very happy times DO and his siblings always looked forward to as they afforded them the opportunity to link up with their kith and kin there. The remarkable thing about these trips is that many other "Kwahu" families resident in other parts of the country also went back home annually. It was a common sight

16

to see "mammy trucks" full of families moving up the scarp from Nkawkaw to Atibie, Mpraeso, Obomeng, Tafo, Nkwatia, Abetifi and Pepease and all the other towns on the Kwahu Ridge. These all received rapturous welcomes from waiting relations. Over time this has evolved into the famed Kwahu Easter celebrations which sees literally thousands of people of Kwahu extraction (including many from the diaspora) return to their ancestral towns for much needed family and community togetherness amid a lot of merry making.

Whenever they visited Kwahu, DO and siblings stayed at Nkwatia. However, it was always the wish of their father Opanyin Kawku Amoafo that his children would not remain in Ahafo (Bechem) permanently. He was keen to see them return to Kwahu and settle in either Abetifi or Nkwatia.

Abetifi became the obvious choice after his father's death in July 1958. The family at Nkwatia was divided over what portion of the properties of their father should go to the children. Eventually most of his properties were taken over by his nephews and cousins.

Fortunately, his father had built a family house in Abetifi to house the 'Ofusii' family. There was also another house, a gift to Nana Odurowaa, so settling at Abetifi was easy for them. Additionally, their maternal family members were mainly in Abetifi and the surrounding villages precisely Nsaree. This explains why they have remained attached to Abetifi to date.

Abetifi is a famous town perched on top of the Kwahu mountains in the Eastern Region of Ghana. It is the Adonten wing of the Kwahu Traditional Area, and the stool belongs to the Ɛtna Bretuo family with the totem of a leopard. Currently the stool is occupied by Nana Asiedu Agyeman III, known in private life as Mr Rexford Kwaku Asiedu, Managing Director of Rasasi Trading Company Ltd. Nana Asiedu was the school mate of DO's second son the late Kwadwo Amoafo and for a long time his business partner.

Abetifi is about 160 kilometres from Accra, the capital city of Ghana and 104 kilometres from the Eastern regional capital of Koforidua. It is 123.4 kilometres from Kumasi to Abetifi. It is well known for its educational institutions, including the Ramseyer Training Centre (for the training of Ministers of the gospel of the Presbyterian Church of Ghana and other church workers), the Abetifi Presbyterian College of Education, the Abetifi Senior Technical/High School, among others. Abetifi is home to the major campus of the Presterian University College, whose other campuses are at Agogo and Akropong Akuapem. The inhabitants feel proud to say that a child born in Abetifi need not travel outside the town for education from kindergarten to the tertiary level.

The Swiss missionary Fritz Ramseyer who played a pivotal role in the establishment of the Presbyterian Church of Ghana (formerly Basel Mission) did a lot of pioneering work in Abetifi and surrounding areas. He arrived in the then Gold Coast in 1864 and undertook missionary work in Kumasi as well as at Anum and Akropong Akuapem. The Ramseyer Memorial Congregation and the Ramseyer Training Centre, both in Abetifi, are among the monuments named after him in Ghana. Abetifi also hosts the Ramseyer Museum, which has a collection of his memorabilia. The building is believed to have been his home in Abetifi for some time before he moved to the section of the town known as "Christian quarters" after the Chief of Abetifi had allocated a tract of land to the Christian community. To the knowledgeable Ghanaian, the name Ramseyer connects more with the town of Abetifi than the other parts of Ghana where this famous missionary worked.

Abetifi is also known for the number of affluent personalities (business people) who hail (and have hailed) from there and the magnificent edifices they have put up there. A notable citizen of Abetifi was the late Mr. P. K. Anim Addo, a business magnate who is on record as one of the greatest benefactors of the University of Ghana. This was at a time when the practice of endowments for universities by individuals was virtually unknown in Ghana.

Abetifi has another claim to fame. At an elevation of 1,972ft (601m), it is the highest habitable point in Ghana. Indeed a monument has been erected at the exact highest point, which is close to the Ramseyer Congregation of the Presbyterian Church. The weather there is most pleasant for the greater part of the year. The Swiss and their love for mountains and the congenial and cool atmosphere they provide may have been influencing factors for Ramseyer to make Akropong Akuapem and Abetifi, both mountainous areas of Ghana, his habitation.

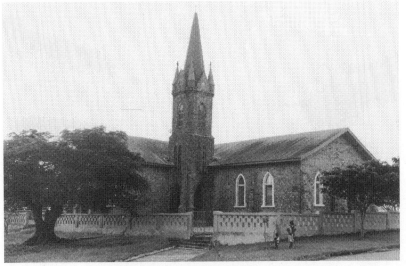

Abetifi Ramseyer Presbyterian Church.

The Journey to Bechem

Human life in the main is not static. One should not stay at one stage of growth forever. *"Sɛ wo te faako a wote wadeɛ so."* His parents, Opanyin Kwaku Amoafo and his wife Awo Akua Dwiraa believed in this adage, so they moved from Kwahu (Abetifi), first to the Akyem Abuakwa area, due to its proximity to the Kwahu area, where they intended to stay and seek their fortune.

They found life tough there so they moved to Asante, after a short sojourn, where the new culture of cocoa farming was beginning to make an impact. They settled at Bechem, now part of the Ahafo Region which was then part of Asante. This was in 1924, before Mr D. O. Amoafo was born.

Bechem was a small town at the time. The town was famous among the Asante for its powerful gods of war. They had their various shrines at various locations in the town. The best known among them were Taa Bekoe, Taa Apem, Taa Dwomɔ. According to history, Asantes never went to war without consulting these gods. Legend has it that Yaa Asantewaa, the famous Asante Queen Mother who led battles against British forces, took refuge at Nyiresua, a suburb of Bechem because of these powerful war gods.

It has since then grown to become a big town of about 20,000 inhabitants with a football club, Bechem United, which plays in the Premier League of Ghana. Bechem is also the district capital of Tano South Municipality.

The circumstances leading to the enrolment of the young Amoafo in school are very interesting and may, at the same time, sound strange to modern day readers. They however shed light on the struggles many of our grandparents and great grandparents faced in their quest for education.

To begin with, his father was convinced that his son was smart and precocious. He therefore always kept the boy close by so that he could be sent on very simple errands. The closeness of the family house to the Roman Catholic Church and the primary school made his education at the Roman Catholic Primary School at Bechem a foregone conclusion. The Catholic Priest and Catechist were vigorously recruiting all the children they could lay hands on into their church and school at no cost to their parents. At the same time, the Presbyterian Church was also recruiting many children, including the older Amoafo brothers into their schools, comprising the lower and upper Primary schools. The competition for children in the small town for schooling among the Roman Catholic and the Presbyterian Church at times resulted in fisticuffs.

DO's father enrolled him at the Roman Catholic lower infant class in 1933. He was only 3 years old. This was because he was not going to spend any money on this initial education, and he must have felt that it would be good to experiment with the situation at the Roman Catholic School.

His first day at the school presented a comic sight. He arrived wearing his mother's vest! Unfortunately things did not work out as his father expected. Apparently, the young Amoafo had also been attracted to the school, but this was due to toffees and other sweets that had been given out to attract the children to the school. The allure of the place petered out after a few days and DO started wishing that he could attend the Presbyterian School at the other side of the town with his siblings. This was the initial objection. The second was the compulsory early morning church attendance by the Catholics before breakfast and before going to school.

After just about two weeks he stopped going to school amidst irregular attendance. The teachers tried to follow up on him through his father. The young boy would run away from the house as soon as he saw a teacher approaching. He refused to return to the school despite remonstrations from his father. The teachers eventually got fed up and they stopped making efforts to collect him from the house. That was the end of his introduction to formal education.

Indeed, this could have been the end of his education completely had it not been for the ensuing developments you will soon be reading.

It turned out that his father, who had showed him much love at this early age, in his hearts of heart, didn't want him to leave his presence. The father therefore agreed that he should not go to school, but should rather be with him to be sent on errands, to help on the farm and to be his constant companion. He gave various reasons for his attitude. He could not understand why all his boys should go to school and leave him alone to his farming activities. Again, he felt lonely in the village (Kwasuogya) where his farms were located because his wife, Awo Akua Dwiraa (DO's mother) was resident at Bechem as a trader in various items. To be precise, she traded in general goods and wares. His father was therefore most part of the year alone with his labourers who were generally from Northern Ghana. They were Grumas, Lolobis, Moshes, Wangaras and Dagombas.

Through this association, he could speak some of their languages. He was fluent in Moshe, Gruma etc. His father found in DO a reliable companion and he sent him to his village instead of the young boy staying with his mother at Bechem to go to school. In the village Amoafo had an older sister, Abena Oforiwaa, who virtually played the mother role. He slept on a mat in his father's bedroom and was a good companion to him in the village. Anyone who needed a favour from his father was sure to receive it if the request was passed through the young Amoafo.

DO spent the week days in the company of his father as the latter went round his farms checking on the work being done by his farm hands. It was a happy-go-lucky time for the lad. There were lots of choice fruits to eat. Exotic birds, some of them now sadly extinct through human activity, were to be seen hopping from tree to tree and chirping away happily. He sometimes found himself howling with delight as the farm hands brought game to his father. These were used for sumptuous palm nut and light soups accompanied with fufu prepared with produce from the farms.

CHAPTER 5

Infant School

After about five (5) years of this "idyllic" life at the village, his mother intervened. She came to the firm conclusion that her husband, Opanyin Kwaku Amoafo, had no intention of sending their son to school.

At about the age of eight and half years old, the lad had become an expert hunter! He had become well-versed in trapping all kinds of animals and using his catapult to shoot at birds with deadly accuracy. Village life and food were very pleasant and easy to come by. He loved it. He dreamt of the day when he would become a man with his wife and children and supervising his own farm labourers.

In June 1938, he followed his siblings who had spent time with him and his father in the village (Kwasuogya) and on the farm back to Bechem. They were returning from holidays to go back to school.

Somehow, the presence of his siblings and the stories and experiences they narrated from school made the young Amoafo yearn to go to school and be like them.

He could read the Twi Primer '*KAN ME HWε*' from Nos. 1 for Class One, 2 for Class 2 and 3 for Class 3. He could also read '*Nsaase Horow so Anansesεm*' (Folklore from distant lands). He could understand a few words and phrases of English. Examples were, "come here, go there, sit down, jump." He could recite the Catechism for Class 1, 2, 3. He had learned these from his siblings whenever they came to the village and farm on holidays.

Young as he was, he had a heart to heart chat with his mother, asking her to approach his father for him to be allowed to go to school with his siblings. His mother, already an advocate for schooling, promptly went to the village to ask Opanyin Kwaku Amoafo to let DO go to school. His father turned down the proposal with sterile excuses, but his mother, Awo Akua Dwiraa stood her ground, at one stage even threatening to leave the marriage if her husband persisted in his refusal.

Faced with this ultimatum, his father agreed, albeit reluctantly, to his mother's request to release the young DO to start schooling. There was however a catch! The old man would have nothing to do with his son's education. He served notice that he would not entertain any demands for school fees or any other things that would be demanded in connection with the boy's education. This threat didn't worry his mother at all. She was already trading with her husband's off-cocoa season funds and was making modest margins through her shrewdness. She was confident that she could cope with the financial demands associated with her son's education. She certainly knew where her strengths lay. Happily, the older siblings had school clothes and basic primers that could be passed on to their brother.

It was against this background that his father, Opanyin Kwaku Amoafo accompanied him and his mother to Bechem, from the village. DO was about to enter a new phase of his young life.

Be that as it may, things were not all that rosy as the young Amoafo started school. DO recalls that when it was time for his father to return to the village, he saw him off to the outskirts of Bechem.

As they parted company, Opanyin Kwaku Amoafo held his son tightly and blessed him with all his fetishes and asked them to guard and guide him.

He made a promise to his father to visit him in the village as soon as the school year ended. All too soon, the end of year holidays arrived and Amoafo and his siblings trooped to the village to spend the holidays there. Each child had his school report on him to show to their father. DO had been promoted to Class two (2) at the end of the year. He had topped his class by a huge margin in grades.

His class teacher, Mr. S. K. Yeboah, was a handsome, fair-coloured man who hailed from Dormaa Aboabo. The teacher had relations at Boama, a town about four miles from the Amoafo village and used to visit them there. The routine he followed was to pass through

Kwasuogya, the Amoafo village, rest for a few minutes and refresh himself with water before continuing his journey on foot.

Teacher S. K. Yeboah knew the young Amoafo and his siblings were spending their holidays in the village and took the opportunity to look the family up. He spent time going through the report of DO with his father and commented on how the lad was excelling at his studies.

Opanyin Kwaku Amoafo became very elated after the class teacher explained the report to him. There and then he revised his stand on the boy's education. DO was nine (9) years old at the time and in class two (2). He still had a lot of hard work to do to enable him to be promoted to Standard 1 (now Primary Class 4) with Class three (3) pupils at the end of the 1939 academic year. He took his studies seriously, took the final exam with Class three (3) pupils and was ranked 3rd. That is how come he found himself promoted to Standard 1 (Class 4), ahead of his classmates.

To his dismay, DO found Standard 1 quite difficult. This was in 1940. He found it difficult to cope with the pace of the studies and the demands of homework. He went into self-doubt, wondering whether he should have stayed in the village with his father after all. He shared his fears with the most senior of his siblings, Paul Oduro Amoafo. Paul was the son of the first of DO's father's wives. She however left the marriage when Paul was barely three years old and the boy was given to the care of DO's mother. DO's mother did a very good job in

28

bringing up Paul as her own child and this explains why the big brother and little brother got on so well even though they came from different mothers. DO told his brother that he could not continue with schooling and that he was returning to his father and friend, Opanyin Kwaku Amoafo at Kwasuogya. Brother Paul (God bless his soul) would have none of it. He pulled his younger brother close to him and spoke comforting words to him. Paul assured him that he would be around to support his younger brother and that he should renege on his decision. This saved the day and DO changed his mind and remained in Bechem to continue with his schooling.

Big Brother Paul proved to be more than a sibling to DO. He was a teacher, friend and mentor. He soon realised that his junior brother had a lot to do to catch up on his studies. Paul took up the challenge to help and devised a strategy for the two of them to sit together after school hours to explain anything DO found difficult in his homework. Paul's persistence, coupled with the teachable spirit and eagerness of DO yielded good dividends. In no time, DO felt comfortable with his studies and looked forward to reporting to school very early each morning to start his classes. His teacher noticed the alertness and bright mind of his pupil and gave him every encouragement. At the end of the school year when results were released, DO ranked third in order of merit. School was now such an enjoyable place to be. He loved the morning assembly sessions, the singing, the marching to the music of the school band and the sporting activities. All the same, it was difficult to let go of the memories of the joys of village life in Kwasuogya, for example, hunting for birds, snails, squirrels and rats, as well as grass cutters. He also looked back with nostalgia to the hunting expeditions at night with his uncle.

Young Amoafo had acquired invaluable knowledge of herbs and their medicinal uses from both his uncle and father who practised herbal medicine for various ailments and conditions that existed in rural life at the time. Looking back, those days in the village (Kwasuogya) could rightly be called 'good' though his verdict now is that it was far better for him to have gone to school.

He is eternally grateful to Big Brother Paul Amoafo who stood his ground and insisted that his junior brother should not abandon school.

 The school was up to Standard Three (now Primary Six) only. Bechem was then, and still is, largely a farming community. Cola plantations were the mainstay of the local economy. Cocoa had just been introduced at the time. Cocoa had been the attraction that drew his parents to Bechem. His father built a house very close to the Taa Bekoe fetish priest house. Maybe he thought he needed protection being a "stranger" from the Eastern Region, a Kwahu man from the mountains who trusted and believed in fetishes. He himself had one, Adade, which he carried with him everywhere he went. It controlled his morality almost all his life.

Front view of the Bechem family house.

Presbyterian Primary School, Bechem.

Catholic Church adjacent to the family house.

Either by design or accident, their house was also located near the Roman Catholic Church and the Catholic Priest's manse. Indeed the property still shares a common boundary with the property of the Catholic Church at Bechem. This made it easy to locate their house. The architecture of the Catholic Church building was in sharp contrast to the old 1925 Amoafo house built with mud-baked bricks.

CHAPTER 6

World War II and Associated Effects

World War II broke out when DO was a young boy. Though just under 9 years old when the war broke out in September 1939, memories from the period are indelibly etched in his mind. Everything changed in the then Gold Coast as a result of the war. The active war years started in September 1939. With the Gold Coast being a British colony, it became enemy territory to the Germans and part of the British military efforts to defeat German Nazis led by Adolf Hitler in alliance with the Japanese.

The impact on the country was immediate and great. Many young men were conscripted into the Royal West African Frontier Force and sent off to fight in India and the jungles of Burma. Some of them were secondary school students, some unemployed and others who could best be described as ragamuffins who were looking for adventure. Some of them got killed in the war and those who came back after the war ended in 1945 were welcomed as heroes. They had many stories to share concerning their adventures in the trenches and their escapades.

World War II also impacted the Gold Coast economically. In the case of cocoa, a lot of the crop was destroyed through officially sanctioned burnings as it was dangerous to ship cocoa overseas. There were reports of German submarines lurking in the deep seas to sink British vessels. A lot of farmers suffered huge drops in income as a result.

DO completed Upper Primary education in 1942. He was to move on to Middle School. Unfortunately, he was compelled to stay at home in 1943. For a period of six months, he was afflicted with an illness with fever-like symptoms. He became seriously ill and could hardly walk. He lost his appetite and this did not help matters. He felt very weak and dizzy all the time. He cannot remember the exact diagnosis of what afflicted him. This period of illness gave his father, a herbalist, a very good excuse to pull him out of school. He explained to his mother that the boy needed at least six months of intensive herbal treatment at the village to recover and recuperate properly. With mother persuaded, DO had no choice but to go back to Kwasuagya village. He was filled with great sadness.

Once in the village, Opanyin Kwaku Amoafo gave the boy all the potions he knew of. Remember that he was a herbalist. For a period of about three months DO ingested potions that were bitter, sour and neutral in taste, three times a day. He had to eat before each medication was administered. It was a difficult period for him as he had lost his appetite. As I write my mind goes back to my own childhood when my mother used to give me and my siblings castor oil. The older readers will certainly remember castor oil. Taking it on a regular basis was not anyone's idea of fun.

Gradually, DO's health improved and he regained his strength. He was now a teenager. Physically, he had hair appearing in his armpits as well as at the lower abdomen. He felt shy whenever anyone commented on how well he was growing. He became more conscious of himself and made sure that he always clad himself well and kept his body clean in every way.

He was out of school for the whole of 1943. His father used him as his secretary and foreman during the period after he recovered from his illness. He became a trader in snails, eggs, onions and finally acted as a shepherd (herder) and rubber merchant. At the age of 13, he was already a businessman.

The year 1943 was the peak of the war years in many respects. The Royal West African Frontier Force was in action in India and Burma. DO, the young businessman, was a supplier of eggs to the Quartermaster at the Kumasi barracks. His source of eggs was the fetish priests and priestesses all over Sekyera (Seikira), Atomfoɔso, Nasana and other villages stretching from Seketia, Drobo to Sampa. The egg, rubber and onion businesses were the most lucrative at the time. The Quartermaster paid readily after he had tested all the eggs on his machine. The good ones were graded and

35

then priced accordingly. DO could at times buy 24 (two dozens) eggs for 6 (six) pence and the big ones for one shilling and sell them for 8 (eight) shillings and 12 (twelve) shillings a dozen respectively. The profit margin was generous. There were risks involved though. For example, accidental tripping of the baskets in which the eggs were carried could lead to their breaking and consequent loss of both cost price and expected profit. Thankfully, such episodes were few and far between. Business blossomed!

The rubber and cocoa trade were his father's preserve. All the same Akwasi Sefa, his father's nephew, and DO had to do the initial exploration and identification of quality products. They would then test them to find out whether they were of good quality before inviting the farmers to bring them to the depot. Herds of cattle were driven from Adadeɛtɛm, along the Sampa-Berekum road to towns like Nasana, Seketia then down to Berekum and Sunyani and finally to Bechem. They were then herded into lots and sold out to butchers and other buyers who were always waiting for them. This was equally very lucrative. DO was involved in all these transactions because he had to issue receipts and render accounts to his father. He performed all these duties at age 13. Can you imagine this happening in this era, reader?

CHAPTER 7

Gathering the Pieces

DO regrets that because of his closeness to his father, he was not exactly a favourite of his siblings for some time. Students of the Bible will doubtless recall the story of Joseph and his coat of many colours and how his brothers hated him because of their father's perceived favouritism towards him. Thankfully, things changed for the better as they all grew older and they warmed up to him, to his relief.

At the end of the year (1943), he had to return to school and his father stayed behind in his village. His father's only brother had died in 1942 and he had to take on many family responsibilities. The machinery for the processing of the rubber and for weighing the cocoa were still at Seikwa which was the centre of the business activities.

All in all, DO's adolescent and senior school years were chequered. Not long after his return to school, his older brother J.A. Amoafo left for the Presbyterian Training College (PTC), Akropong Akuapem. Paul Oduro Amoafo and the other siblings were all at various stages of schooling. With World War Two taking a heavy toll on the economy and with cocoa beans being burnt for lack of market, things were tough for his father. Indeed this was an experience shared by many others in the West African sub-region. As indicated, a lot of young people had also joined the army to fight the war on the side of the British.

On his return to school in January 1944, he found his classmates in Standard 5 (Middle School Form 2). He was made to join his juniors in Standard 4 (Form 1). At the beginning, he felt uncomfortable. He felt like a fish out of water and could not move freely with his new classmates. His previous mates who were now ahead of him by a year would also not accept him, or so he felt. There were some embarrassing moments.

DO also found the academic work very challenging. His one year absence from school seemed to have made his mental faculties suffer somewhat. He found many of the lessons difficult to understand. Mathematics and English were particularly problematic. English proved to be very difficult because he couldn't understand the English at all. Some of the textbooks used were by Lacombe and Longmans. They might as well have been written in Greek or Arabic, as far as he was concerned. He could not make head or tail about anything written in the books. Yet he was expected to complete assignments given by his teacher from the books. All was not lost though. He came across alternative books by Simon & Miliken which had worked examples on the topics being treated in class. He took to working out problems in Mathematics following the examples and gradually his understanding of the subject improved.

At first he felt ashamed of himself, but his determination to succeed paid off. One of the strategies he adopted was to seek help from seniors he considered bright. He also applied himself studiously to his books, making the most of his time. He was indeed preparing to cross the bar! Subjects such as Hygiene, Nature Study, Geography, Civics and Bible Study fell into his grasp easily but English and Mathematics were difficult, as already indicated.

When the end-of-year results were released, DO was among the top ten best performers in his class. The teachers who knew him in Primary School were happy that he had bounced back.

DO soon caught the eye of the Headteacher, Mr. J. F. Ako Larbi (Master Ako), who did not fail to notice the boy's neat school uniform and clear handwriting. He was very neat and always had his hair and nails nicely trimmed and manicured. Master Ako engaged him to copy down his notes into a big Note Book he kept. Master Ako, an Akuapem man from Abiriw, was a very disciplined and organised person. He was also a great musician and Choir Master in the local Presbyterian Church. DO still has fond memories of him.

By the time he got to Standards 6 and 7, the last two years of elementary school, he was enjoying his studies thoroughly. He felt at home in most of the subjects offered. English continued to cause a few problems, with him sometimes mixing the tenses. Things to be committed to memory did not give him problems, but verbs which had to to be in agreement with the subject proved to be tricky. Long poems in English were memorised easily and could be recited back to front (bottom up).

It was not all books, however. DO was a member of the Boy Scouts movement. He recalls with nostalgia the camping expeditions he and other Boy Scouts made into the forests and the tents they pitched to sleep in at night. On starry nights, they would huddle together and share Ananse stories. His hunting skills from Kwasuogya came in handy on those occasions and he led his fellow Scouts to trap small game and crabs which they barbecued over open fires made from twigs and branches of trees. They knew how to kindle a fire without using matches. A lot of life skills were picked up through those experiences. Sadly, these are now things of the past. He hopes and prays that they will be reintegrated into extra-curricular activities in our schools to enable our young people learn much needed life skills.

"I was a very smart member of the Boy Scouts in my days," to use his own words.

CHAPTER 8

Precious Waiting Time

DO completed his Middle School Education in 1947. He then became a pupil teacher for a year, from January to December 1948. This was because his father was not in a position to finance his secondary school education at that time. Based on his performance in school and in the Middle School Leaving Certificate examination in which he secured a Distinction, the Presbyterian Minister at Bechem, Rev. Kissiedu, thought he could become a good teacher. The Reverend Minister was of the view that DO could be prepared for the teaching field by employing him as a pupil teacher. That would set the stage for him to take the entrance examination to enter the Presbyterian Training College (PTC) at Akropong Akuapem to train as a professional teacher. His elder brother, J.A. Amoafo, had finished his Teacher/ Catechist course in 1948 at the same College.

While his brother J. A. Amoafo was waiting for his posting, he had information from the Presbyterian Church Headquarters in Accra that he and some colleagues had been awarded scholarships to undertake a Secondary School Course at Krobo Odumase. The institution involved was the Presbyterian Secondary School (Presec), which was relocated from Krobo Odumase to Legon about 21 years later. His brother spent two years at Presec studying for the Cambridge School Certificate. This meant that DO had to hold on to entering secondary school as his father could not afford to pay school fees simultaneously for his two children while catering for six other children in elementary school.

Rev. Kissiedu posted DO to Mabang where he served as a pupil teacher at the Presbyterian Primary School. He was in charge of Class One.

Mabang was about two and a half miles away from Tepa, now District Capital of Asunafo South in the Bono Region. Among his pupils was Mr Ellis Owusu Fodwor, a well-known criminal Lawyer. He loved his pupils, played with them in the sand, sang and played the tennis ball barefooted together. He still has a sense of nostalgia whenever he sees Primary Class One pupils.

From Mabang he was transferred to Nyiresua to be part of the pioneering staff of a new school. What a challenge that presented! The young DO was however not perturbed and was determined to do what he could to succeed. The Headteacher of the new school was called Mr Oppong. He had been DO's senior in Middle School and hailed from Kwasu, which was a few miles from Nyiresua.

The two villages (Kwasu and Nyiresua) had to provide everything needed to make the school succeed. A lot of community spiritedness was displayed by the inhabitants of the two villages. The Chiefs and Elders of the villages recognised the benefits a school would bring to their children and mobilised their people to support the Presbyterian Church to get the school off the ground. Land was provided and communal labour went into erecting the structures. Chairs, tables and all miscellaneous school logistics like registers, chalk and Teachers' Note Books for classes were provided by the Church and elders of the two villages. These and many more were provided. The District Minister from Bechem paid visits to inspect the progress of work and was satisfied that the two villages were ready for the school.

Then came the day for the inauguration of the school. What a glorious day it was. DO still remembers the day. The Chiefs and people of the two neighbouring villages to benefit from the school assembled. Rev. Kissiedu, District Minister of the Presbyterian Church at Bechem came with his Elders and the Church Choir. The Church Choir sang an anthem which brought an air of solemnity to the proceedings. There was a lot of drumming and dancing. Reverend Kissiedu (the District Minister) read Psalm 127 from the Bible and said prayers to dedicate the school and blessed all those who would pass through the walls of the institution. Psalm 127 says that *"unless the Lord builds the house, those who build it labour in vain"*. There was an air of expectancy and anticipation. At the end of the formalities, everyone went home, happy to have been present to witness such a memorable occasion. Please bear in mind, my dear reader, that having a school in a "remote" part of the Gold Coast in those days was a huge affair and something everyone who was involved in making it possible felt very proud of.

The elders of the community had to accommodate and feed DO, a task they discharged cheerfully. The Headteacher, Mr Oppong, was a native and already resident in the village. Their salaries were cumulated and paid at the end of the year. This arrangement did not present any hardship as the young DO had virtually all his meals taken care of by the community in addition to free accommodation. Nyiresua was about three miles away from Bechem so he was able to move between the two places at his convenience.

In the meantime, many of his school friends had gone to various Secondary Schools in Cape Coast, Accra and to PTC. So he made it a point to make new friends at Nyiresua, especially. These friends were not educated. They found in DO a teacher to help them to read and write at least. The "Mass Education" programme was at its embryonic stage at the time. It was a joy to see the pride on the faces of many of these hitherto illiterate friends as they learned to read. Some of them became Bible readers in Church.

CHAPTER 9

Prempeh College, Abuakwa State College, Presec and PTC Akropong Akuapem

DO kept in touch with his friends at the various secondary schools and particularly at PTC, Akropong Akuapem through correspondence. Letter writing was one of the surest ways of keeping in touch with loved ones and acquaintances in those days. Mails were delivered to Nyiresua from the Post Office at Bechem once a week on Thursday afternoons. Everyone was full of expectancy on Thursdays, hoping for a letter from a friend or even a pen pal in another part of the world. This was in sharp contrast to the delivery of telegrams which always brought bad news of the passing away of a loved one. One of the friends DO corresponded with regularly was called Koo Boateng. He encouraged DO to leave no stone unturned so that he could go to secondary school.

An opening soon came when DO got admission to Prempeh College, Kumasi. This was in 1948, when the now prestigious school was admitting its fresh batch of students. He was however not impressed with the school when he arrived on the campus. Prempeh College, a joint venture of the Presbyterian and Methodist Churches, had just started in an abandoned army barracks.

He therefore opted for Abuakwa State College (Abusco) at Kyebi in the Eastern Region. That was in 1949. He was in for a disappointment. He became disillusioned soon after he arrived at the school. The environment was worse than what he met at Prempeh College. There was also a lot of bullying ("homoing") of new students. The bullying he encountered at Abusco, he says, was too much and even posed a danger to the safety of new students. It was too "brutal."

It is worth noting that DO was able to fund his entry into secondary school from his accumulated savings as a pupil teacher. His father was pleased that his son had enough savings to pay for the fees and gave his blessing to DO to enter secondary school.

After just one academic year, he left Abusco to continue at the Presbyterian Secondary School (Presec) at Krobo Odumase. He entered Presec in 1950. He felt more at home there, even though conditions there were quite spartan. He was however comfortable with the Presbyterian structures and discipline at Presec. Another plus factor for Presec was that his elder brother J. A. Amoafo (his role model and lookalike), had established himself as one of the best products of the school at the time. He wanted to tread in his brother's footsteps. While at Presec, DO got to know the surrounding areas, including Somanya and the Akuapem Ridge quite well as the school took students on regular hikings and sporting activities in the countryside. He completed his Cambridge School Certificate Course at Presec in 1952.

From Presec, DO proceeded to the Presbyterian Training College (PTC) at Akropong Akuapem to train as a teacher. This was after he had passed a competitive entrance examination.

The circumstances surrounding his going to Training College were interesting. PTC had not been his preferred destination. He had hoped to proceed to sixth form at one of the schools offering Advanced Level courses and had taken a special entrance examination towards that objective. He was confident that he would make it and follow his elder brother J. A. Amoafo to St. Augustine's College in Cape Coast. Thereafter it would be a natural progression to University. His brother had distinguished himself as one of the best students at St. Augustine's College (just as he had done at Presec) and had gained admission to the University of Ghana, Legon, then domiciled on the western compound of Achimota School. It was therefore natural for him to aspire to enter university through the same route.

Against all expectations, DO failed to gain admission to any of the sixth form schools, which were at that time mostly in Accra and Cape Coast. He therefore accepted an offer from PTC to train as a post secondary teacher. He had delayed for almost one term before going to the College, hoping against hope that he would receive a call up to sixth form.

The term had almost come to an end. He was enrolled at PTC exactly two weeks to the end of the first term. Needless to say, he had a lot of catching up to do. By dint of hard work and a lot of self-denial he was able to go through the course.

DO's memories of PTC are good ones. To begin with, the weather was cool and clement like that of his hometown Abetifi. The buildings there were of solid blocks and concrete and the compound was very pleasing. Fruit trees and other trees were dotted over the compound with beautiful landscaping. His teachers included Mr. Fred Agyemang, who later became Director of the Ghana Institute of Journalism. Fred Agyemang in later life established himself as a literary expert, author and Church historian. Fred Agyemang and D. O. Amoafo were later to meet and worship together at Dansoman Emmanuel Congregation of the Presbyterian Church of Ghana. DO's College mates included S. K. Apea, M.A.C. Addo and George Sakyi Aburam, who all rose to high executive positions in various establishments. S. K. Apea (also from Abetifi) for example, became Deputy Managing Director of the then Social Security Bank (now Societe Generale Ghana), Deputy Governor of Bank of Ghana and Deputy Minister of Finance in succession. George Sakyi Aburam became Managing Director of Social Security Bank and M.A.C. Addo rose to become a top executive at the Volta River Authority (VRA). Another classmate was Anane Frimpong, who became a lawyer. Another teacher was the Rev Otto

Boateng, a great church musician whose compositions were taught to the College students. Yet another teacher was Mr Kwabena Nketia (later Emeritus Professor), who later became a legendary figure in ethnomusicology and brought a lot of honour to Ghana. Sundays saw the whole College assemble in the stone chapel for church services. The students also learned to sing songs by Kwabena Nketia and the legendary Ephraim Amu (Owura Amu) who had been sacked as a tutor at PTC by the missionaries for daring to mount the pulpit to preach in a traditional attire, a Kente cloth. Suffice it to say that this fascinating personality brought so much inspiration to us as Ghanaians and Africans.

Yes, PTC was a happy experience. One of the things DO enjoyed most was when the students were sent on teaching practice. This saw them distributed to schools in Akropong, Abiriw, Dawu, Mamfe, Larteh, Adukrom, Apirede and other towns on the ridge for periods of up to three weeks every term. There were three terms in the academic year. He passed out of PTC in 1954 with the Teachers Certificate A.

DO was all this time pursuing correspondence courses to improve upon his chances of entering university. He did this through self-tuition materials from University Correspondence, Wolsey Hall, Bennet College and others.

These courses helped him to obtain four passes at the Advanced Level. By 1958, he had passed in Economics, Economic History, History (British) and British Constitution.

DO recalls that he had also studied Latin through the same correspondence courses. However, he did not write the examination out of fear that he might fail. It was after he took a look at the questions after the examinations were over that he realised that his fears had been unfounded. Judging from the questions and the state of his preparedness, he told himself that he would have excelled in Latin if he had taken the examination. It was however too late.

CHAPTER 10

Marriage and Family Life

At this stage, he was more than qualified to go to University. This was in 1958 but he held on till 1962. This was attributable to two main reasons. He wanted to go to the United Kingdom to read law. That had also been his father's vision for him.

The second, and more important one, was that he had got married in 1956. The marriage to Victoria Margaret Boatemaa Diawuo (later Mrs Margaret Amoafo) was not preceded by any period of courtship. How could this be? To the uninitiated, this was normal in those days. It was customary for parents to agree on spouses for their children.

His father was by now a rich cocoa farmer who was ready to provide every support to his son. He was also determined to see his children married to people of Kwahu extraction as a way of ensuring that they did not remain in Bechem but went back to settle in Kwahu. DO had to get married. His father wanted to see a wife by the side of his son.

Margaret's father, Opanyin Kwabena Diawuo and DO's father, Opanyin Kwaku Amoafo were friends. Both of them belonged to the Asona clan. They had been thinking of spouses for their children and at one stage Margaret's father went to introduce his daughter to Opanyin Kwaku Amoafo. Without saying much, both fathers knew, instinctively, that their children could forge a union. Opanyin Kwaku Amoafo in particular felt convinced that this was the woman his son needed. He did not waste any time. He sent for the young DO and told him that he had found a wife for him. It was as simple as that.

Did DO object? No! He was persuaded that his father knew best. With that, a date was agreed for the performance of traditional marriage rites between the two in 1956. It was a Saturday afternoon at Abetifi and Opanyin Kwaku Amoafo, in the company of a number of family members went to the family house of Opanyin Kwabena Diawuo and sealed the traditional rites with drinks and money along the lines stipulated by Kwahu custom. DO was not even present. He was not required to. He was waiting patiently at home till it was all over and his wife was brought to him in the evening. Ten years later, the marriage was blessed under ordinance at a beautiful wedding ceremony held on July 23, 1966 at the Abetifi Ramseyer Congregation of the Presbyterian Church of Ghana attended by family and friends. Mrs Alice Adarkwa Dadzie, one of the witnesses, who has since become a family member through close association with the family, still speaks about that day and how the wedding of the Amoafos was the talk of the Abetifi township.

Wedding Day – July 23, 1966 Ramseyer Congregation, Presbyterian Church of Ghana, Abetifi.

DO was at the time of the traditional marriage a teacher at the Dormaa Ahenkro Presbyterian Middle School, where he had established himself very early as a young hard working teacher. Margaret proved to be industrious, supportive and humble. Margaret, who to DO's grievous pain departed this life on Sunday, August 18, 2019, proved to be a real pillar of support to her husband. They had been married for over 63 years at the time of her death. In his tribute to her, DO admitted to mourners the difficult times Margaret had to endure as a wife. He referred to the many times he had gone wayward as a husband and how she had remained resolute to the sustenance of the marriage. This was attributable to a decision Margaret made at the onset to build her marriage and remain steadfast in it whatever the obstacles that arose.

DO was very forthcoming and candid about his character flaws as he recounted his life story. He regrets that he did not live up to expectation and caused pain to people close to him, especially his wife Margaret. In his own words, he caused a lot of pain and chaos to his peers, family, friends, community and by extension the nation in various ways.

DO admitted to having breached his marital covenant by fathering two of his nine children outside marriage. This caused Margaret a lot of distress. He said that his days at university were the worst in terms of his social life.

According to him, he allowed the freedom of university life to overwhelm him. He had gone to university as a mature student with financial independence, unlike most others, and he took advantage of his access to the fast life to indulge in habits he is not proud of. He took to drinking, he says, and to hanging out late with some friends and engaged in activities he would not be proud to mention or recommend to any young person.

DO is however grateful for the grace of God which found him and rescued him from the perilous cliff of destruction he was slipping into. He is ever grateful to the salvation he found in the Lord Jesus Christ, which brought him out of darkness into the marvellous Light of God. By grace, he turned his back to drinking, bad company and immorality.

In recounting those horrible days, DO never ceases to thank his late wife Margaret for her patience, long-suffering, endurance and support in spite of all that he did. As Proverbs 31:10 says, *"An excellent wife who can find? She is far more precious than jewels."* This is how DO describes his wife, whose long-suffering and warm-heartedness made her forgive her husband and encouraged him to move on despite what happened.

He ends by saying that while such temptations may come one's way as a young man, it is important that one comes to one's senses and return to God for one's own sake and eternal destiny.

DO and wife, Margaret Amoafo.

Mr. & Mrs. Amoafo at Dormaa Ahenkro.

Margaret Amoafo

DO's late wife, Mrs. Margaret Amoafo was the only child of her mother, although her father had children from other marriages. She was the eldest of all her siblings.

As the only child of her mother, the latter advised her to keep her marriage at all costs and give birth to as many children as she could to expand her family base. She was therefore very determined right from the onset to accommodate every situation to maintain her marriage no matter the challenges. Her mother, Maame Ama Yeboaa and later her adopted sister Abena Asabea, committed themselves to support her in caring for and raising all the children to adulthood. Mrs Amoafo on the other hand, followed her mother's advice and she committed herself to hard work; submission and respect for her husband and her in-laws. She embraced her husband's family and nurtured the young ones among them as her own. Her children's friends and their neighbours all took her as their mother. By the Grace of God her dream for a large family was fulfilled. Between the two of them they were blessed with nine (9) children and all the children's names have been provided at the end of this chapter.

She was very prayerful and occupied herself most of her time with church activities. In particular, she took her fasting and prayers very seriously.

Early years of Mrs. Margaret Amoafo at Dormaa Ahenkro.

Margaret (Mrs. Amoafo) as a chorister.

Mrs. Amoafo poses for the camera after Sunday service.

By the nature of his teaching career, DO was transferred from place to place every now and then. At each station, his wife supported him and the family that came later by engaging in trading activities to supplement the family income.

In addition to his job as a teacher and in typical Kwahu fashion, he operated a convenience shop at Dormaa Ahenkro, his first station after graduating from PTC. This he left to the care of his wife since his teaching activities took most of his time. According to DO, the shop prospered so much that he and Margaret attracted envy and enmity from some members of the community. Indeed he felt so alarmed for their safety that he applied for, and was granted, transfer to Kumasi.

In Kumasi, he taught at the Adum Presbyterian Middle School. His best known students there were the Baffuor-Awuah twins, Kwame and George. Kwame and George became the first set of twins to be admitted to the University of Ghana Medical School, in 1971. Kwame remembers DO as a strict and serious teacher who wanted to see his pupils well grounded for success. He was also not one to spare the rod for naughty students. He went the extra mile to prepare them for the Common Entrance Examination. Through his tutoring, Kwame and George passed the examination and gained admission to Prempeh College, from where they proceeded to the University of Ghana.

The Baffuor-Awuah twins went on to establish two well-known clinics in Accra. These are the First Foundation Clinic at Dansoman, owned by Dr. Kwame Baffuor-Awuah, who has over the years become an institution in the Dansoman community and the second, Mt Sinai Clinic owned by George. Unfortunately, George has passed away. Kwame testifies about the impact DO made on their lives and told me, when I interviewed him, that he will never forget the contribution of DO to his life and that of his brother.

While at Adum Presbyterian Middle School, DO was looking for a good place in Kumasi to move his store to from Dormaa Ahenkro and enter university. This proved to be difficult, contrary to what he had expected. He was forced to keep the store at Dormaa Ahenkro till 1962 when God, in His own wisdom, permitted two events to occur which made it easy for DO to proceed to university.

This is what happened. Within the space of one week, he lost both the store and his energetic storekeeper.

The storekeeper fell ill on a Friday evening and by noon the following Sunday, he was dead. He had used a lot of the funds of the enterprise to procure goods and merchandise from Kumasi on the Friday. He went on to deliver a sizeable portion of the procured items to retailers at Dormaa Ahenkro on credit the same day. He was going to update the books with the details the following Monday. Then the unexpected happened.

He died on Sunday and no creditor would own up as having received any supplies.

In the event, DO lost both the storekeeper and the store. The store collapsed and he decided not to resuscitate it. These two events are what "forced" him to embark on his previously delayed plans to enter university.

The store business had been good while it lasted. With prudent management and investment, he had savings of over £20,000 in his bank account. He believes that he was the richest of all his father's children at the time. Due to the collapse of the store and losses occasioned by it, he used a substantial portion of his savings to pay off his debts. He then gave what was left to his mother who topped it up to build the family house at Abetifi.

The first child, Divine Kofi Boama Amoafo arrived in 1957. In 1958, the second child, Kwadwo Amoafo, arrived without any complications forty days after the death of DO's loving father. He named the baby after his father and christened him 'Comforter', but as he grew, Kwadwo did not like the name and hardly used it. Kwadwo did not like the name because people mistook him for a girl whenever they saw it. Indeed when he entered Mpraeso Secondary School, the school authorities thought he was a girl and placed him in a girls dormitory!

This is the full list of his children, each now well settled in life with their own families.

Divine (Kofi) Boama Amoafo, Comforter Kwadwo Amoafo (deceased), Cynthia Asare Bediako (Mrs), Wisdom Anim Amoafo, Michael Osei Amoafo, Omega Dwira Amoafo, MyraStella Ansah (Mrs), Kwaku Amoafo, Stella Dwiraa Amoafo

Look at what the children have to say.

The children, now all grown up and established in their careers and with their own families, recall with nostalgia how privileged it felt to grow up under the care and protection of their father. DO was a hard task master who felt that only the best was good enough for his children. At the same time he was a lot of fun and very loving.

The children remember that he was not one to compromise on high standards of discipline. He insisted on good personal hygiene for each of them and saw to it that each child, and indeed every family member in the household, kept themselves clean, dressed smartly and maintained well trimmed haircuts and finger nails. They also had to pass through his "School of Handwriting."

DO demanded the best performance from his children, and provided a home environment which was conducive to learning. They, the children, reciprocated and always strove to do their best. He always showed his approval for a good performance by patting them on the shoulders and telling them to keep soaring like the eagle. Where he was extra happy with the performance of any of them, the child in question would receive a special gift. At other times, the reward would be a good portion of meat from his afternoon fufu meal or a ride to school after the afternoon break. The psychological boost the children got from such car rides to school was immense and powerful as being given a ride to school was extremely rare in those days. In those days there were afternoon breaks in school which allowed school children to go home and return after an hour. Some children in some homes across the country were known to be made to pound fufu and perform other chores like fetching water during those breaks. Fortunately the Amoafo children were spared these labours.

His eldest son, Kofi Boama (who now lives in Australia, having previously been resident in New Zealand) and his siblings are grateful to their father for ensuring that they acquired life and social skills in addition to the academic side of their lives. They are also particularly grateful that their father brought them up in the fear of the Lord.

On the life and social skills side, DO got them involved in extra-curricular activities such as playing table tennis, football, piano lessons and typewriting. DO used to invite school children and young family members to join his own children to play games. He used the opportunity to advise them to take their studies seriously. With football, he even tried to establish a colts club with his friend Mr. Foligah, though this venture did not did not really get off the ground.

On the spiritual side, Kofi Boama recalls how their father, with the support of their mother, introduced them to Bible study, prayers and fasting. DO established a family altar and the whole family fasted and prayed on Wednesdays and Fridays. Needless to say, attendance at Sunday church services was mandatory. They have grown up to become mature and discerning adults and parents as a result of the solid foundations their father (and mother) gave them.

Growing up, one of the things that intrigued the children, and others, was how DO named his children when they were born. When they were in school, their friends used to ask them if their father hailed from the Volta Region, given the descriptive way people from that region give first names to their children. Their answer then was in the negative. However, now that their family and historical links with Kpando in the Volta Region have been established, any such questions now will be met with a yes answer.

As indicated, one of the things which fascinated them, when growing up, was how their father named his children. They now understand that they were named to match his spirituality, the occasion surrounding their births and also to honour some close relations who had made significant impact on his life or in the wider family.

There was always history behind each name. Kofi Boama was named after DO's uncle (his father's only brother)

Yaw Bimpeh. The uncle's real name was Yaw Twenefuor with Boama-Koteakro as his accolade. Somehow, earlier children who were named after him with Twenefuor died in their infancy. The Twenefuor was therefore discarded and DO's eldest son was named Boama, with Divine as his first name to ward off any evil spirits. The second boy, Kwadwo Amoafo, was christened Comforter as he was born not long after DO's father died and he was meant to symbolise the comfort DO needed for the pain of losing his much loved father.

Cynthia, the brain behind this book, was a sign of joy and represented the "moon" to DO on the arrival of his first daughter. Cynthia is called Maame Yaa by many in the family because she was named after his aunt Yaa Asabea Tawia. Cynthia was born exactly 40 days (and on a Thursday) after DO's aunt died. The two boys after Cynthia, Anim and Osei, were both named after his uncles, brothers of his mother Awo Akua Dwiraa.

Omega was named after his mother. Similarly, each of the rest of the children, Omega Dwira, MyraStella, Kwaku Amoafo and Stella Dwiraa were named after his father and mother and in the case of MyraStella, his mother-in-law. MyraStella is therefore known as Maame Yaa Yeboaa.

DO's children are happy that they have made him proud in their various fields of endeavour. They are engineers, career civil servants, businessmen, chartered accountants and veterinary doctors. What more could a father wish to see of his children? They are full of praise to their father for his compassion, sense of duty, insistence on hard work, making the right choices and his sheer passion for life.

Kofi Boama and his siblings will forever treasure the family times together at DO's various teaching posts at Apam, Peki and Koforidua. The times at Abetifi and Dansoman are especially precious. They still remember DO helping them with their school work and teaching them nursery rhymes. They also remember the times they spent in the balcony at Dansoman, as they grew older, playing draughts and scrabble with him.

Above all, they are proud of the legacy of a good name passed on from their father which opens doors for them wherever they go in Ghana.

Celebrating DO at 80, a pose with children; Stella, Anim, Cynthia, Omega, Kwadwo, Osei, and Boama.

Mr. & Mrs. Amoafo with Cynthia and grandchildren Michael, Papa, Noami and Nana.

CHAPTER 11

University and Work

Having secured all the grades for admission to university, DO finally entered the University of Ghana, Legon. He was a proud resident of Legon Hall, the premier Hall of Residence.

At Legon he studied History and Economics, graduating with a Bachelor of Arts (BA) degree in 1966. What a commendable achievement, considering where he started from. From Kwasuogya to Legon was indeed a confirmation that what God has destined will surely come to pass!

After graduation from university, he went back to teaching. He had been granted study leave with pay for the duration of his studies and returning to the classroom was the right thing to do. He was posted to Apam Secondary School, where he taught History and English Literature. Those were the golden years of Apam Secondary School as a centre of scholarship, under the headship of Mr P. A. Owiredu.

After Apam came a period at the Peki (Avetile) Government Training College (GOVCO), from where he headed back home to Abetifi to teach at Abetifi Presbyterian Training College (ABETICO). His stay at ABETICO was short and he soon found himself transferred to the Abetifi Presbyterian Secondary School (APSEC) where in addition to classroom duties as a teacher of History and English Literature, he was a House Master and acted as Assistant Headmaster. His students at Abetifi Presbyterian Secondary School have fond memories of him and credit him with moulding their characters and giving them solid foundations for life. They were present in their numbers at DO's 90th birthday celebrations. Some of the goodwill messages to him on the occasion are reproduced in Appendix 2.

Quick transfers then followed after Abetifi, first to Koforidua, to the Eastern Regional Education Office as an Education Officer and then to the Greater Accra Regional Education Office. It was at this point that he moved the family from Abetifi to Accra, specifically to Dansoman (Sahara).

DO had not given up his aspiration to read law and he saw his transfer to Accra as fortuitous. He applied to study for the Qualifying Certificate in Law (QCL) at the Ghana School of Law and was accepted. He started attending lectures and invested in a number of textbooks. According to him, his bosses were not happy that he was trying to read Law and transferred him, out of turn, to Ho. The transfer to Ho effectively put an end to his legal studies as it was impossible to attend classes. He felt extremely disappointed and wrote to the School of Law to withdraw from the course. Among his course mates was the late Mr Nuhu Billa, a senior Police Officer. From Ho, he was transferred back to Accra and posted to the Textbooks Unit of the Regional Educational Office.

The posting to Accra saw the family move to the Dansoman Estate where DO and his family spent many fruitful and happy years. This is with special reference to the Dansoman Emmanuel Congregation of the Presbyterian Church of Ghana, which he joined with his family. Dansoman Emmanuel, as the congregation is popularly known, had started barely a year before DO moved to the community. He thus became one of the "early Fathers" of the Church and played key roles, including becoming an Elder and father figure to many. In a bid to encourage members who lived in his neighbourhood to grow in their devotional life, DO opened his doors to a home cell group which met at dawn on week days to pray and meditate on the Word of God. That gathering led to many testimonies about answered prayers by members.

By 1970, DO and his wife Margaret had a family of six boisterous, intelligent and handsome boys and three very intelligent and lovely daughters. It was a happy home and Margaret was the matriarch who ensured that everything, from feeding, cleaning and house chores, went well and according to plan. The routine in the home, especially from dawn when everyone had to assemble for morning devotions before getting ready for the day's activities, resembled that of a military barracks.

To be a teacher and parenting nine active boys and girls in a revolutionary Ghana was no joke. DO gives credit to his late wife, Margaret, for their success in raising their children. He describes her as one who had a real determination to carry her family through the rough and tumble of life and stand by her husband and children come what may. She was the matron and bursar of the home.

Through diligence and shrewd planning, they always had enough to eat and to spare. DO and his wife ensured that each of their children had what was needed for school and church. He put his children through good secondary schools: St. Peters, Mpraeso, Aburi Girls', Presec (Legon) and Accra Academy. He ensured that they had everything they needed for their studies.

DO has always believed in the biblical admonition in Proverbs 22:6 to train up a child in the way he or she should go, so that they would not depart from it when they grow, and he did exactly that. Among other things, he drummed it into the ears of his children to shun bad company, telling them that bad company ruins good morals (1 Corinthians 15:33). The teaching paid off and the children were extremely careful in whatever they did. They chose friends who were from similar backgrounds. Some of them learned typing and secured vacation employment at the Greater Accra Regional Education Office during their student days.

In 1982 DO retired voluntarily from the Civil Service. As a Kwahu man he wanted to go back to his roots and do what his kinsmen are known and respected for, business. Indeed, this was what had motivated, even if indirectly, the prosperous business he had established at Dormaa Ahenkro at the start of his teaching career. He was 52 years old in 1982 and decided that it was best for him to retire voluntarily at a time when he still had a lot of energy. He told himself that if he waited to retire at 60 before venturing into business, he might not have the drive and energy needed.

He took his retirement package and moved to Koforidua to team up with his friend Mr Kwaku Baah who was in the logs and lumber business. He had had the opportunity to observe the business line at close quarters during the time he worked at Koforidua, where he had been posted on transfer from Abetifi in 1974. He had also spent time learning about the personal experiences of Mr. Kwaku Baah and had come to the conclusion that this was a viable business proposition to pursue.

The two friends went into sawn timber business, selling timber products at the Koforidua timber market. DO's family was now settled in Accra and he shuttled between Accra and Koforidua, mostly on weekends. Unfortunately, after few years he realised this business was not thriving the way he had anticipated and came to the conclusion that it was best to call it quits and cut his losses rather pumping more capital into it. This was the period of harsh economic conditions in Ghana, principally occasioned by a severe drought which hit Ghana in 1983. He moved back to Accra to join his family. He registered a sole proprietorship with the name A.O. Daniels. The main business line of A.O. Daniels was the supply of hardware and hospital consumables to the Korle Bu Teaching Hospital and other government institutions.

Fortunately for DO, he almost always ran into some of his students at the government institutions he approached to do business with. Those from APSEC in particular were delighted to be of help to "Oluwa" as they had nicknamed him during their student days. Some of his students from APSEC and other schools in Kumasi and Dormaa Ahenkro were even heading some of the institutions he did business with and they were always ready to be of assistance to him. He managed this successfully, though it was on a small scale .

In the late 1990s he felt that it was time to take a final bow from active working life and handed over the business to his son Kwadwo Amoafo to take care of. In early 2000, DO and his wife retired to their Achimota home and devoted the rest of their time to church and family affairs including grand parenting, something which gave them great joy.

The last born, Stella, a very clever girl passed the Common Entrance examination in Class 6. While preparing to enter secondary school, she won a Government of Cuba scholarship to study in Cuba for 11 years. She came back with Msc in Accounting and Finance. She is now a Chartered Accountant and one of three Partners at Intellisys Ghana, having previously worked with Deloitte Ghana and PZ Cussons.

DO is extremely pleased that his children turned out well and are married and spread across various parts of the globe. He has no doubt that they have their own stories to tell, which they will do at the right time in the future.

At the same time, he is still getting over the sudden and unexpected death of his second child, Kwadwo Amoafo in 2017. This was a big blow to DO and his wife, Margaret. Indeed his wife never recovered from the shock of Kwadwo's untimely passing away till her own death barely two years later in 2019. Kwadwo, businessman, philanthropist and family person had been a life wire for the "Amoafo Clan" and his sudden and unexpected death brought untold sorrow to DO and the whole family.

DO ready for lectures at the University of Ghana (1964).

CHAPTER 12

Travel and See!

DO has led a full life. The experiences he feels particularly thankful to God for include his trips to various parts of the world. He never misses an opportunity to make references to these. As I keep saying myself, life is made of memories. One should therefore make a conscious effort to build pleasant memories.

The early 2000s saw DO and his wife travelling the world, literally, to visit their children, friends and relations abroad. The trip had been planned in such a way as to end in far away New Zealand, where their eldest son Divine Kofi Boama and other family members are resident.

This was their first overseas trip and the first time they were travelling by air. Stella and other siblings in Ghana were at the Kotoka International Airport to help them through immigration and offer last-minute guidance on cabin etiquette. They first went to the United Kingdom (*aburokyire*) where they visited their adopted daughter Lily and her husband Yaw Okraku. The journey was planned to offer them a good opportunity to see other parts of the world while at the same time saving them a very exhaustive long haul flight to New Zealand. As such their first stop was London in the United Kingdom (UK) arriving at the Heathrow airport early morning with British Airways. They were waved through immigration by very friendly immigration officers and as they entered the arrivals hall, their son-in-law Yaw Okraku was waiting for them. Lily and Cynthia had been school mates since infancy. Through this relationship, DO and Margaret adopted Lily and her siblings into their family circle and they have remained close family members since then. DO and Margaret spent two weeks in the UK staying at Tottenham in London with Lily and her husband. The couple's son Kwasi Okraku had arrived a week earlier. DO and Margaret had planned their arrival in London to coincide with the naming ceremony as they were going to be the godparents. The naming ceremony was a beautiful one, and had a number of family members and friends resident in London present. DO felt proud at the honour done him and his wife.

While London had been meant to be a transit point in the original scheme of things, it turned out to be very memorable and packed with a lot of activity. It was very enjoyable, and for senior citizens who grew up in the Gold Coast at a time when what is now Ghana was a British colony and Britannia ruled the waves, there was a nostalgic twist to it. They went on sight-seeing visiting places of interest including Madame Tussauds, London Bridge, Westminster Abbey and Piccadilly Square. They had a lot of fun riding on the London City Hop on Hop Off Tour buses, sitting in the upper decks of the double-decker buses. DO was excited to see so many historic places he had read about while he was studying in secondary school, Training College and at University. DO is grateful to Mr. and Mrs. Nkansah Frimpong who sponsored the London City tour. Mr. Nkansah Frimpong is the son of the late Very Rev. I. H. Frimpong, a former Moderator of the Presbyterian Church of Ghana.

DO's nephew, Kwame Safo, who was also resident in the UK paid them a visit. DO and his wife had supported Kwame Safo in school in Ghana and the reunion was a very happy one indeed.

While in the United Kingdom, they travelled by coach to The Netherlands to visit their daughter Cynthia who was doing graduate studies at the Institute of Social Studies (ISS) at The Hague. Cynthia had Dutch family friends by name Leo and Tony Van Leeuven and they were happy to host her parents in their home at Ridderker for a day to enable them have a taste of a traditional Dutch home experience. Interestingly, the couple had met two of DO's sons, Osei and Omega, in New Zealand the year before, while on vacation there. There are no coincidences in life, I keep saying. Meeting DO and Margaret was therefore a pleasurable experience for Leo and Tony Van Leeuven.

On hearing that DO and Margaret were on their way to New Zealand, Leo and Tony recommended places of interest they felt strongly that DO and his wife should visit while in New Zealand. They also visited various places of interest in The Hague that they had heard about, including the International Court of Justice. In Amsterdam the couple visited Groeneveen, the site of the 1992 cargo plane crash; which involved a number of Ghanaians and Africans and the monument raised in their memory.

They then took the Euro Channel express train to Brussels, in Belgium, on a return trip to tour the city. The plan was to have the Euro Channel experience and also visit some historic sites in Brussels and surrounding areas before returning to the UK. In Brussels they had a look at the EU headquarters, the popular Manneken Pis, a landmark bronze fountain, and a few more monuments and tourist sites before going back to The Hague. They returned to London by coach, content and ready for the next leg of their world tour.

DO and wife in London.

At an underground Tube Station in London.

In London at Madame Tussauds. Encounter with Arnold Schwarzenegger.

Madame Tussauds with Fidel Castro.

The US Trip

From London, they flew across the Atlantic to Boston, Massachusetts, in the United States. They were met at Logan airport by Mr Tetteh Cobblah (brother-in-law of their eldest son Divine) and his wife Liz.

From there, they were taken to the home of the Tetteh Cobblahs in Maynard, Massachusetts. Maynard is a suburban town in Middlesex County, Massachusetts, and is about 22 miles west of Boston.

Maynard is renowned for the production of digital computers, and it is also a historic mill town. DO was particularly interested in the history of Massachusetts so they visited historic places in town, such as the Old North Bridge, spanning the Concord River in Concord. They stood on the bridge that stood between the British colonial soldiers and the armed farmers (Minutemen) who fired the first shot in defiance of British authority and rule. This is what started the American War of Independence in 1776.

They visited Harvard University and Chapel Hill-Chauncy Hall School, an elite school in Boston, where Anoff, son of the Tetteh Cobblahs, was a student and watched his last basketball game of that season.

They were also driven through Wellesley College, the famous all women's college where Hillary Clinton, the Secretary of State in the Obama administration, had her undergraduate education.

While with the Tetteh Cobblahs they were made to feel very much at home with Ghanaian and American foods during their stay.

They thoroughly enjoyed their time with Mr Tetteh Cobblah (brother-in-law of their eldest son Divine) and his wife Liz and children in Massachusetts.

New Zealand, Here We Come!

Their final destination was New Zealand where they spent some very memorable times with their eldest child Divine Boama Amoafo, his wife Eileen and family as well as their two other sons, Michael Osei Amoafo (and his wife Freda) and Omega Amoafo.

Their time in New Zealand (NZ) was truly memorable. By the time they arrived in Dunedin, they had literally travelled as far away from Ghana as they could, for the simple reason that Ghana and New Zealand are virtually opposite each other on the International Date Line.

Dunedin is the second largest city in the South Island of New Zealand (after Christchurch) and is the principal city of the Otago region of New Zealand. Its name comes from Dun Eideann, the Scottish Gaelic name for Edinburgh, the capital of Scotland. Dunedin was settled by the Maoris in the 1300s and the Europeans arrived on the shores of Port Chalmers in 1848. And today it is said that there are no real full-blooded native Maoris left in New Zealand.

Their eldest son Kofi Boama, his wife Eileen and their three young sons (Kwadwo Opong, Kwabena Asare and Kwabena Yeboa (twins) were living in Dunedin at the time. Two other sons, Michael and Omega were in Christchurch. The primary purpose of this trip was to get away from the social demands and pressures back home and spend quality family time with their families in Dunedin and Christchurch. In particular they wanted to have special times with their grandchildren. They also used the opportunity to undergo thorough medical reviews.

They visited a number of historic and interesting places in Dunedin and surrounding areas in the Otago region. The town is home to the historic Larnach Castle. The Royal Albatrosss Centre, a large wildlife sanctuary offering an observatory, exhibits and guided tours is located in Dunedin. The port of Port Chalmers and the Moeraki Boulders with their unusually large and spherical boulders known to be caused by the breaking tide on the Koekohe beach are also to be found in Dunedin. They managed to visit all these places as well as Baldwin Street, reputed to be the steepest residential street in the world according to the Guinness book of records.

While in Dunedin they met with Bill and Clare Hodgson who had lived in Ghana in the 1960s when the Korle Bu Hospital buildings and residential flats were being constructed. Bill had been posted to Ghana from Nigeria, where he had completed a similar assignment, to supervise the building construction works by the State Construction Company (SCC). DO and Margaret struck a friendship with the Hodgsons that lasted long after they returned home.

They also visited a number of tourist attractions in the historic towns of Queenstown, Wanaka and Alexandra all in the Central Otago region. Queenstown is the adventure capital of NZ. They went on the gondolas that took them to the mountain tops to take in the vista of the lakes. The region is also known for its picturesque scenery, Victorian architecture, orchards and wine making. They enjoyed the trip through these new and different places.

While in Dunedin, they made other trips around the South Island of New Zealand. They also went to Christchurch to spend time with Michael, his wife Freda, their new grandchild Yaa Boatemaa and Omega.

Their stay in Christchurch was fun and they met many friends of Osei and Freda. One of such persons was the then Moderator of the Presbyterian Church of New Zealand, The Rt. Rev Bruce Hansen. He was the parish minister of the local parish where they worshipped.

On their way back to Dunedin, they made a two-day road trip through the west coast of New Zealand. This was an interesting trip as the area is rugged and has a tropical rain forest, similar to what we have in Ghana. This trip took them through towns like Hokitika (a popular town known for its wild food festivals) Wanaka and Queenstown, prestigious skiing towns in New Zealand and popular tourist sites.

Margaret stayed in New Zealand for an additional month after DO left for Ghana.

DO and his wife forged some lasting friendships from this "world tour" of the year 2000 and these have remained in touch through correspondence and telephone calls since then. What they particularly enjoyed during those trips was being able to spend extended periods with their grandchildren who did not live in Ghana. They did not hold back from any opportunity to "spoil" them, even if this displeased their children. They returned to Ghana truly fulfilled. I remember him telling me about some of the places they went to, after we had closed from church one Sunday.

Mr. & Mrs. Amoafo at Knox Presbyterian Church in New Zealand.

Mr. & Mrs. Amoafo 's visit to the Christchurch Botanical Gardens, NZ.

In Dunedin on a Sunday morning after Church.

In Dunedin, NZ with grandson, Oppong and Boama's friends (Fred and Tracey Painting) after afternoon tea.

Mr. & Mrs. Amoafo spending the afternoon on the veranda in Wanaki, Central Otago, NZ.

Mr. & Mrs. Amoafo in Dunedin, Early Settler's Museum.
With grandchildren, Asare, Yeboah and Oppong.

Afternoon walk in the park with the family in Dunedin, NZ. Oduraa, Mrs.
Amoafo, Asare, Eileen, Yeboah, Boama, Oppon and Nana DO.

Mr. & Mrs. Amoafo on the observation tower. The gondolas in Queenstown, Central Otago, NZ.

CHAPTER 13

Providential Escapes from Death

The fascinating story of the life of DO cannot end without a recall of a few unusual incidents in his life.

DO remembers vividly a terrible experience he had as a five year old boy. He was feeling particularly hungry one late morning. For some inexplicable reason, breakfast had delayed. He saw a pot of freshly cooked cocoyam, yet to be dished out and in his desperation, he took one cocoyam from the pot to eat to kill his hunger and wait for his standard portion. He was not fast enough. His mother's rival, Yaa Bosuo, caught him in the act and chased him to snatch the cocoyam from his little hands. As he tried to escape, little DO fell and a sharp stick he was holding in one hand pierced his throat. He fell down heavily. Those around who saw what was happening went to his aid and managed to pull out the sharp stick from his throat. A grievous wound had opened up and the blood was flowing freely through his nose and mouth.

Three days later, he woke up with indescribable pain. His head and face were badly swollen and he was in such bad shape that his father was afraid for his life. His father promptly sent DO to hospital, where he received good attention and medication. Thankfully, he recovered well after about two weeks, with the wound fully healed.

DO ascribes his escape from the untimely death or at best disability that could have arisen from this incident to divine providence. He believes, strongly, that the grace of God and angelic visitations have been his portion throughout his life. What else could the explanation be for this and other dramatic and unexplainable episodes in his life, he asks rhetorically?

He goes back into memory lane to the year 1942 for another incident. He was in Primary Class Six (6) and World War Two was raging. The Gold Coast was a key supplier of goods to the British war effort. Consequently, shipping lines from the Gold Coast and other West African countries became a target for German submarines, as already indicated. Indeed there was also the fear that there could be aerial attacks on land from the planes of the dreaded German Luftwaffe!

Lights were dimmed to conceal towns and storage depots at night. Cocoa was bought at the cheapest price and later burnt because there was no market for them. Schools were not to conduct evening classes except for Class Six (6) and Standard Seven (7) under tight conditions.

The pupils were allowed to attend evening classes with either candles or 'Kwatash' or "bobo" a locally made lamp which was fuelled with palm oil.

Somehow he fell asleep in the classroom after classes ended one evening. His brother and the others who were there left for home without realising that DO was asleep. Somewhere in the deep of the night, he woke up suddenly to the glare of a very bright light he cannot find words to describe. After some seconds which seemed like eternity, the light disappeared. He was shaken with fear. Nevertheless, he mustered courage and left for home in the dark. When he narrated what happened the next morning, everyone thought he had just had a nightmare. That experience made him fall sick for about six months. He believes that it was some evil force that had attempted to harm him but that he had been saved by the hand of God. He testifies that divine providence has been at work in his life, judging from the motor accidents (as many as six serious ones) he has escaped unscathed from. Psalm 91 has been his declaration as a result of these near escapes from death.

"He who dwells in the shelter of the Most High will rest in the shadow of the Almighty. I will say of the LORD, He is my refuge and my fortress, my God, in whom I trust. Surely he will save you from the fowler's snare and from the deadly pestilence." Psalm 91:1-3 NIV

He encourages all to to put their trust in the Lord God Almighty for their own good.

DO encourages the young people of today to set their sights high and work assiduously towards the realisation of their goals. He is persuaded that the Lord God Almighty knows the plans He has for each and every one of us. *"These are plans for good, not for evil, to give us a future and a hope"* (Jeremiah 29:11). What is needed is for each one to be serious in life and make the best use of the opportunities that come all the time. God has given us brains and talents, but He expects us to apply them towards the achievement of our plans and goals.

He is pleased to testify that God has been his Helper and that without the help and protection of the Lord he could never have crossed the bar and lived to share his story. He ascribes the glory for whatever he has achieved to the grace, mercy and favour of God.

May God bless everybody who takes the high jump of life and to His name be the glory and everlasting joy, DO says.

CHAPTER 14

Insights from Extended Family

In my search to find out more about DO, I asked his daughter Cynthia Asare Bediako if there was an older family member I could speak to. Cynthia directed me to Mr. Lawrence Benjamin Amoafo, a younger brother of DO. After finding out that he lives in Akim Oda, I reached him and set up a telephone conference with him.

I had a number of questions for Mr Lawrence Benjamin Amoafo or Uncle Badu as he is called by his nephews and nieces. Badu is the name given to the tenth born child. We had a very interesting conversation. Uncle Badu has been resident in Akim Oda since 1973. He first arrived there when he was transferred by his then employers, Ghana Library Board, from Keta to their branch Library in Oda. After a few years in Oda, he took early retirement and established a drug store which later became a full fledged pharmacy, Labeamo Pharmacy and which is still in operation.

Uncle Badu is an Elder of The Church of Pentecost. He credits his brother for directing him to join the Church at a time when he was a young man with a lot of worldly desires. This was in the year 1963.

Uncle Badu states that DO and his elder brother J. A. Amoafo, were role models to him and the rest of the young people in the Amoafo family. DO was a brilliant student with excellent handwriting, he told me. He described his brother as jovial, friendly, respectful of others including those much younger than him. DO has always been very kind and caring, he stated. He made sure that in addition to his own children, he sponsored other family members to secondary school. He is God fearing, he said, and that always made him concerned about the wellbeing of others.

Uncle Badu credits his becoming a Christian to his brother DO. According to him, he was into occultism as a young man. This had been a matter of concern to DO who sent Uncle Badu a long and strongly worded letter advising his younger brother to give up occultism and give his life to Christ. The letter made a deep impact on him and he decided to visit DO at Apam Secondary School, where DO was then a teacher, to discuss matters with him. When he got to Apam DO was not there, having travelled to Accra at short notice.

Paradoxically, his not meeting his brother at Apam made Uncle Badu even more desirous of taking action on the advice DO had given him. Soon after getting back to Takoradi, where he was schooling, Uncle Badu attended a revival meeting organised by The Church of

Pentecost and responded to an altar call to give his life to Jesus Christ. He has not looked back since.

Uncle Badu narrated two other incidents he has never forgotten. The first was when, as Boy Scouts Captain, DO led a Boy Scouts delegation to a Scouts Conference in Lagos, Nigeria. On his return, DO brought along a bottle of sea water back home to Bechem. What is special about this, you may be asking at this stage? The fact of the matter is that no one in the family and in the school at Bechem had seen the sea before, much less sea water. DO caused a stir as he displayed the sea water which the children, adults and many others gazed at in wonder.

That story reminded me about something I heard when I was in secondary school about the first time some of our compatriots from the hinterlands of Ghana saw the sea. They were reported to have been so mesmerised by the wideness of the sea and the roaring waves that they are said to have asked if they could cook "mankani" (cocoyam) in it! I am not going to mention which tribe they belonged to, and I shall not tell you if you track me down to ask me.

The second incident was in March 1966, not long after the military coup which overthrew Dr. Kwame Nkrumah, Ghana's first President. He, Uncle Badu, was having his wedding in Sekondi. It was a grand wedding which coincided with a regional convention of The Church of Pentecost. He remembers this very clearly.

Five Amoafo brothers (including DO) and three sisters drove all the way to Sekondi in two cars to support their brother. On the eve of the wedding (which was held on a Sunday), a Saturday evening, the siblings were on their way to Takoradi to see someone when one of their vehicles got into a collision with another vehicle at a T-Junction. One of the brothers got out and gave the occupant of the other vehicle a hefty slap which saw the driver fall into a nearby drain. Unknown to them, the other driver was an Army Officer, a Captain. He was in the company of another officer. He got up from the drain and the two drew pistols on the Amoafos. It was a most frightening experience. Fortunately, they did not pull the triggers. After some exchange of words, the Amoafo siblings went to lodge a complaint with the Police and at the same time made a desperate telephone call to the late General M. A. Otu in Accra to complain about the misuse of weapons by the officers. According to Uncle Badu, they later heard that the officers were punished severely.

On her part, Professor (Mrs,) Comfort Charity Atuahene has a very personal testimony about DO. According to her, DO is her first cousin, brother and mentor, all combined into one.

DO is her cousin because they are both descended from the same great grandmother, Abrewa Nyarkoa. He is her brother because he is her mother's sister's son. He is her mentor because during the time she was growing up in Abetifi, DO was held in very high esteem and she was one of the young people who looked up to him. DO was one of the very few in Abetifi at the time who had had university education. Indeed, she recalls that there were only four university graduates in Abetifi at the time. Whenever these four came to Abetifi, both during their student days and after graduating, they would usually be seen walking together. The townsfolk, especially students, admired them a lot and they were known as the ones who had been to "sukuukunini" the Twi term for the grandest educational institution.

Professor Atuahene remembers how she and other young people aspiring to enter university in the future would peep through their windows just to have a look at the four "musketeers" and would be wondering what they could be conversing about.

When it was time for her to get married, the man who proposed to her came from a tribe other than the Kwahu tribe. This was contrary to the expectations of her wider family. They were not amused and there was great opposition to the proposed union. When DO got to know of the opposition, he took the trouble to sit the family members down and persuaded them, or so it seemed, to accept the marriage. A date was therefore set for the marriage ceremony and family members gave an indication that they would be present in their numbers.

Then came the day for the marriage ceremony. Contrary to expectations, they failed to turn up!

The only people her husband to be came to meet were DO, her parents, the Minister of the Presbyterian Church and the Elders of the church. None of her other siblings showed up. Sensing embarrassment, DO stood up boldly and announced that he was going to accept the marriage on behalf of the family and all the siblings. DO made it clear that he was prepared to take responsibility for the consequences. With that, the ceremony proceeded and ended on a beautiful note.

Professor Atuahene relishes the fact that DO was proud of her because she was one of the few females, if not the only one, from the family to have had university education during that period. One needs to bear in mind that girl child education was not a priority for many parents at the time. It was because DO was so proud of his cousin for her educational achievements that he had stood up for her during her marriage ceremony in order to save her from disgrace.

She feels a profound sense of gratitude to DO for his prayers for her and his blessings on her to have the best marriage in the family. In God's providence, these prayers and blessings bore fruit. She testifies that she has had one of the best marriages in the family.

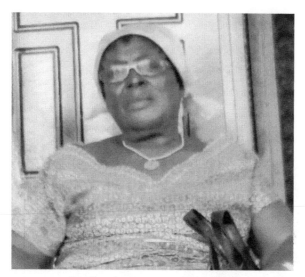

Paulina Anyanewaa, DO's sister.

DO's sister, Comfort Amoafo (Adusa).

Mr. Lawrence Benjamin Amoafo (Uncle Badu), youngest brother of DO.

CHAPTER 15

Abetifi Presbyterian Secondary School (APSEC)

Some of the most fruitful times in the life of DO were those he spent teaching at Abetifi Presbyterian Secondary School (APSEC).

His students are unanimous in their verdict that he made a lot of impact on them and the school for the few years that he served as a tutor and later as Assistant Headmaster. He worked under Mr. C.K Ceasar the Headmaster and briefly under Mr. E.O. Saka, who came in at about the time DO was leaving APSEC. Some of the staff he worked with included Mr. Michael Ofori Mankata, Miss Susana Lokko, Mr. Tekpetey, Mr. Okleme, Mr. Asamoah, Mr. Afiademango, Mr. Sintim Brown, Mr. Thomas Lartey, Mr. Adofo, Mr. Victor Coopewazer, Mr. Owusu Banahene, Ms Lydia Addi, Mr. D S Boateng, Mr. Ohene Darko, Mr. Glover, Mr. Foliga and Ms. Barbara Hall of the United States Peace Corps. Another notable colleague was Mr. Kwasi Ampadu, who later became Headmaster of the Akropong School for the Blind. He was very good at reading the Braille and teaching it to blind students.

Being a native of Abetifi, it was his desire to help build the school academically for it to compare favourably with the likes of St. Peter's Secondary School and Mpraeso Secondary School, the two leading schools on the Kwahu Ridge at the time.

He was very much devoted to his teaching and would go the extra mile to ensure that all students in the school were disciplined in their behaviour and academically serious.

Abetifi Presbyterian Secondary School was at that time located at the original site which was right in the heart of town. The school was housed in private buildings and close by were family houses with many odd activities that could easily cause distractions to the students and affect academic work. One of the dormitories for boys was quite far from the school premises and was nicknamed "Biafra." The students in this dormitory had to walk through the town centre to and from school each day through many a potential distraction. It is on record that none of them had the courage to misbehave, loiter in town or go wayward. This was because they were always under the eagle eyes of DO, who they nicknamed "Oluwa." Oluwa lived close by, and they could never tell when he would call anyone straying to order and to certain punishment (caning) the next day at school assembly. DO remembers the names of some of the students, in addition to those whose messages of congratulations are reproduced in Chapter 17.

Samuel Nii Odoi, Emma Abdullai, Helena Gyamfuaa, Alex Ofosu Ampadu, O.O Larbi (deceased) were some of his students at APSEC. The late O. O. Larbi married his niece Janet Osei (also since deceased). DO believed that his students should know how to use their hands in addition to their heads and hearts. He made sure that the students took part in extra curricular activities. Apart from the standard sporting disciplines, he led the students to engage in farming activities. By a fortunate turn of events, this was when the late General I. K. Acheampong was Head of State and Chairman of the National Redemption Council (NRC) in Ghana. As all the world knows, General Acheampong rolled out a policy called "Operation Feed Yourself" which enjoined Ghanaians to capture the commanding heights of the economy, as he put it so beautifully. This meant that institutions, families and individuals were to use all available arable land to plant food crops and other economic plants to enable us improve on our lives. DO galvanised his students with this message and led them to establish maize farms to feed the school. In addition, he saw to the planting of teak trees along the Abetifi-Abene road by the students. Needless to say, his childhood experiences as an "Okuraseni" (villager) at Kwasuogya had prepared him for this.

You will doubtless recall the young hunter from Kwasuogya too. With the trap setting skills he had honed in Kwasuogya, DO set traps along a stretch of land of about 20 acres. These yielded a round the year supply of bush meat for family and friends. Everyone wanted to be his friend, in the hope that they would get portions of the bush meat for their fufu eating sessions. DO did not disappoint. What nostalgic memories!

He was very much loved and appreciated by his students at APSEC who found in him a tutor, a disciplinarian, Christian and friend.

The Administration Block (New Site) at Abetifi Presbyterian Secondary School (APSEC).

CHAPTER 16

More Abetifi Memories

Beyond the fact that Abetifi is DO's hometown, the town holds a special pride of place for him and his family. This is principally due to the time he spent on the teaching staff at Abetifi Presbyterian Training College (ABETICO) and Abetifi Presbyterian Secondary School (APSEC) which we just read about in the previous chapter. But there is more!

DO taught at ABETICO briefly before moving to APSEC.

It was at ABETICO that he formed an enduring relationship with a colleague teacher by name Mr. Boatey. This teacher hailed from Krobo Odumase, where DO had completed his secondary school education at Presec. Boatey, a Fine Arts teacher, was in need of accommodation and asked DO if he knew of any place available for renting. DO readily offered him a place within the family house he had constructed with the proceeds from his savings after he had paid off his debts on the Dormaa Ahenkro shop.

The two teachers forged a very cordial relationship and in no time this warmth trickled down to their wives and children.

The then newly constructed house was comfortable and modern by all standards in those days, even though electricity had not yet been connected to Abetifi at the time. Indeed electricity from the national grid was not connected to the town till around 1973.

Boatey's wife and children were back in Krobo Odumase during his time at Abetifi. The first long vacation after their father moved into the Amoafo family house, the Boatey children came to Abetifi on holiday. The children of the two teachers hit off so well that their fathers agreed on an "exchange programme" for subsequent holidays. From then on, every long vacation saw the Amoafo children in Krobo Odumase while the Boatey ones went to Abetifi.

Cynthia Asare Bediako still remembers how thoroughly they, the children, enjoyed those holidays and how they got to know other parts of Ghana through the travelling involved.

Aunt Elizabeth, Mr. Boatey's wife (now deceased) and sisters Maku and Georgina were extra nice. Being a Fine Arts teacher, Mr. Boatey committed himself to keeping the Abetifi house and surroundings very nice and neat. He decorated the lawns with white stones. These were very exciting times and DO's children are grateful to him for providing them these and other opportunities they still look back to fondly.

The long vacations were like the Kwahu Easter celebrations of today. They were very happy times. The Amoafo family house was always full with boisterous teenagers. There were lots of household chores like fetching water from the stream Nkawkwade, seeing to the poultry farm, going to mill their food. The children also took turns to sell wares on the streets of Abetifi and hawking food to the teachers who did not have their families with them. Later the girls and boys started rotating for the Krobo Odumase and Abetifi trips. Each time the boys from Odumase came to Abetifi the girls would go to Odumase and vice versa.

Boatey helped to organise table tennis competitions in the Abetifi house which soon became a popular recreation centre for the students of Abetifi.

Life was so simple and very enjoyable. A lot of that was attributable to the "Amoafo factor." DO's nephews and nieces were always in the house and forged close relationships with his children. Cynthia remembers that their cousins were their seniors and in various secondary schools. They served as motivation to the Amoafo children to aspire to pass the Common Entrance Examination and enter secondary school. The Amoafo children have maintained excellent relations with their cousins. Cousins like Osei Wiafe, Osei Ampadu, Kwame Osafo, Yaw Asomani, Janet and Margaret Osei were and have always been with them, on both happy and sad occasions. In Cynthia's case, her late cousin Kofi Amoafo (the eldest of the cousins) asked that she resit the examination because, in his opinion, she did not select first class schools. She did so the following year and gained admission to Aburi Girls' Secondary School, certainly one of the best schools in Ghana. In the event, she had a very happy and successful time at Aburi Girls' and, as I write, she is the immediate Past National President of the Aburi Girls' Old Students Association.

The bonding in the Abetifi home was not restricted to the children, their cousins and their friends from Krobo Odumase. The Amoafo family home had ample space and the wives of two of DO's cousins Adusei Poku and Kwasi Nyarko also lived there. These two, Beatrice Yeboah and Beatrice Nyarko, were teachers at the Anglican Primary School. They and their sister-in-law Margaret, DO's wife, had a very cordial relationship and contributed to creating a lively, highly enjoyable and satisfying atmosphere for the Amoafo children and their cousins. Such large family settings were common in those days and helped children to acquire much-needed social skills before they were sent off to secondary (boarding) schools. This may be contrasted to the small nuclear family settings of the current times with family members doing everything possible to protect their turfs and keeping in touch mostly through social media. The close relationship continued till DO's wife Margaret passed away in 2019.

CHAPTER 17

DO turns 90

The 90th birthday of Daniel Opong Amoafo fell on Monday, January 6, 2020. The occasion was however celebrated on the following day, Tuesday, January 7. As explained in the Introduction to this book, the celebration on January 7 was to allow as many loved ones as possible to attend, the day being a national holiday. The 90th birthday celebration was a grand affair. This was a day DO had been looking forward to following his 80th birthday celebrations a decade earlier. At the time of his 80th birthday celebrations, the 90th had sounded far off and uncertain.

What a joyful event it was! Present were the surviving siblings of DO, his children, grandchildren, in-laws, family members from Nkwatia and Abetifi, neighbours and friends from the Achimota Salvation and Dansoman Emmanuel Congregations of the Presbyterian Church of Ghana.

It is worth pointing out that a lot of people were technically left out of the invitation just because the occasion had somewhat been overshadowed by the sudden death of DO's wife Margaret in August 2019. In a partially mourning mood, the planners decided to restrict the numbers and have a closed family celebration. But the love so many people have for DO, his associations and large numbers of acquaintances made this almost impossible.

The event planners, Mawuse Waka and Michael Asare Bediako (iamadinkra), were at their best with their creative and artistic decorations and live video coverage. The entire atmosphere was charged with good wishes, joy and melodious songs. The CLOGSAG band from the Ghana Civil and Local Government Service provided very inspirational and beautiful gospel, high life and old "skuul" renditions. The 90-year-old celebrant could not remain sitting down and got up to dance merrily to the melodious tunes.

Lyns Ventures, owned by his daughter-in-law provided a magnificent three-tier well prepared and decorated cake to celebrate him. Food and drinks were in abundance, thanks to Evelyn Ayete and Bridgett Catering Services.

What a joyful event it was! Present were the surviving siblings of DO, including Prof. Comfort Atuahene, his children in Ghana, a cross section of his grandchildren, sons in-law (Mr. Kwasi Bediako and Kingsley Ansah), family members from Nkwatia and Abetifi, neighbours and friends from the Dansoman Emmanuel Congregation and the Salvation Congregation (Mile 7) of the Presbyterian Church of Ghana.

There were also special delegations from the Aburi Girls' class of 1980, the Alumni of Cuba students, special adopted family friends including Mrs. Levina Owusu, Ms. Margaret Bosomtwe, Mrs. Gloria Apenkwa, Ms. Eunice Akosua Ofosua Amoako, Mr. Kofi Ampadu Boateng. Abusua Mr. Dankwa and his team, and many more. Other very close friends who could not make it to the place for very good reasons sent their recorded video messages and well wishes. These recordings included that of his sister Paulina Anyanewaa Amoafo, (she was present though) who used the opportunity and the occasion to thank God for blessing DO to live up to 90 years. She recounted the time, long ago, when she had to join her husband in Accra, and DO and his wife Margaret came to take over from her in taking care of their family home at Abetifi. She wished him well and prayed that his wish of going up to 100 years would be granted by God. She prayed that all such years would be full of good health so that he would not be bedridden.

Madam Beatrice Lartey of the Dansoman Emmanuel Congregation of the Presbyterian Church of Ghana, was happy to be associated with the event. She was thankful to DO for helping her to become strong in the Lord through the Prayer cell in his Dansoman home and especially for her being able to evangelise to others. Above all, she was extremely grateful to DO for taking her as a daughter (Asona ba) and supporting her in extremely difficult times. She recounted how DO helped her to bury her dear brother by accompanying her to her hometown and assisting her to go through all

117

the traditional rites. She was very grateful and wished him more years and God's blessings.

Madam Mary Yirenkyi, also of Dansoman Emmanuel and formerly with the School of Performing Arts, University of Ghana, was not left out. She also recounted how DO assisted her to go to school in the UK, specifically to Leeds university, to study for her Masters degree, by getting Cynthia to take care of her house and her two young family members. She was very grateful for that gesture and wished him more years filled with good health and God's blessings.

Mrs Margaret Banful, a neighbour and friend who shares the same birth year (1930) with DO also spoke. Her birthday is in April and they call themselves classmates, she said. Because she is also called Margaret, they have struck a very close acquaintance and quite often after church (they both worship at the Achimota Salvation Congregation) they would meet and enjoy Presbyterian hymns and pray together.

Kofi Ampadu Boateng, a younger friend who has become a member of DO's family could not contain his joy seeing his father turn 90. He prayed that all his other wishes would come true just as the 90th had come to pass.

Each speaker praised DO for his impact on their lives through his love and caring nature. The fun-loving side of DO was brought to the fore by all the speakers and his cousin Kofi Poku Adusei in particular referred to his sense of humour and his "sweet tooth." It was so much fun interspersed with soothing music with lots to eat and drink. Mention was also made of his prayerfulness and how he and his late wife Margaret impacted many lives through the home cell that functioned at their Dansoman home and other places. Joseph, his adopted son, used the occasion to thank him for picking him from the street and bringing him to his home. He was very thankful to him and his late wife whom he affectionately calls Abrewa. The opportunity was also given for neighbours to express their wishes. It was indeed a very solemn but hearty celebration.

His students were not left out. They paid glowing tribute to their teacher on the occasion of his 90th birthday and prayed for many more healthy years for him. The icing on the cake was the symbolic presentation of gifts from a cross section of the participants. Notable among them were the gifts from the family, Aberewa Nyakoa descendants, the children, grandchildren, sons-in-law, (Kingsley Ansah and Kwasi Bediako) daughter-in-law (Kate Boatema) and other close associates. It was simply beautiful!

DO took turns to take photographs with all the individuals and groups present. He made sure that he interacted with everyone who made it to the celebration.

When he was given the opportunity to speak. DO thanked everybody present and those who sent him messages for the show of love. He advised that the love and concern shown to him on his birthday should not be for just the occasion but must continue for all time.

119

He advised that it was always good to show love and so all those who had come to his party must go back and demonstrate love to others.

The tributes reproduced here are from some of his students at Abetifi Presbyterian Secondary School, where he was a teacher, Housemaster and Assistant Headmaster in the early 1970s.

Yaw Kusi also known as Yaw Martin (1972 group) writes:

"Mr Amoafo was my mentor and inspiration. He taught English literature in a way that made the subject easy. Amidst the unexpected turmoil in 1972, he was a pillar to lean on and I remember he guided and supported me while looking for a place at sixth form.

Congratulations, Sir, on your 90th and I pray you live happily in the coming years."

S. Asiedu Sasu writes:

"I would like to pay tribute to Mr Amoafo, for he had a significant impact on my life and education. His tutorials and advice during my time at APSEC were very helpful which has made me what am today. God Bless you."

E. O. Amankwah, Assistant Senior Prefect (1970) writes:

"MY BIRTHDAY TRIBUTE!!!!

Yes, I can vividly throw my mind back to the 70s, when you walked in almost daily to teach us English Literature. Our set Books were: Animal Farm, Macbeth, Silas Marner and of course the Almighty Chaucer: the Prologue and the Pardoners Tale. I remember the D. O.

Amoafo, neatly dressed in short sleeves shirt and a corresponding trousers. Of course I still picture you with your bushy hair.

Yes, those were the days, the good old days of D. O. Amoafo and E. K. Caesar.

Today as you celebrate your birthday, I say with pride that the totality of all that you did for us is what has made me today. I have a daughter here in London and she's so so proud to have me as a father more so when I quote from the Literature Books I read almost 50 years ago.

DO I'm so grateful to have been one of your students. My command over the English Language is all down to you, your commitment, dedication and all that you did 50 years ago to make APSEC a place worthy to talk about.

As you celebrate your birthday it is my wish that the Almighty Father will make it a joyful occasion ever to be remembered."

Agya Dane (Philip K. Osafo, a nephew) writes:
'Hello DO,
You are ninety years today. What a milestone. We give thanks to the Almighty God your creator. Do you remember telling me ' Kwame am going to be 92 before I hand over the baton? Your words have come true. 90 and 92 I see no difference. You are there. I never took it seriously it would come to pass. That was 1971. I am very grateful to you for making it possible to attend APSEC.

That was a quantum leap in my life. When all hope seems to fade away you gave me that opportunity. No amount of words can I summon to thank you. May the Lord give you more strength and years to hit a century. Amen."

DO at 90

DO cutting his 90th birthday cake.

DO tasting his birthday cake with the help of Kate, Cynthia and Stella.

DO dances to his happy birthday music.

Do with grandchildern.

DO with Anyanewaa (Sister), Kofi Anim, Stella and Cynthia (children).

*DO with siblings and cousins. Anyanewaa seated, Comfort Amoafo (Adusa),
Prof Atuahene (cousin) and Kofi Opoku (cousin).*

DO with in-laws.

DO receives a gift from family members represented by Margaret Sekyere and Kofi Opoku.

Michael and mum Cynthia sharing a toast.

DO responding to toast.

CHAPTER 18

The Role of a Mother

This book has been written not merely to recount the life history of Daniel (DO) Opong Amoafo, but also to serve the bigger and more important purpose of being an example and encouragement to the up and coming generation of young people (and the not so young) to live up to their full potential and become useful citizens.

In this connection, I deem it particularly important to reflect in more detail, on the Role of a Mother in the lives of her children using the example of Obaapanyin Akua Dwiraa, mother of DO, as a reference point. Our mothers have not been celebrated enough. Indeed it is only in recent years that the celebration of mothers has been elevated through the annual Mother's Day and the United Nations Day for Women. Even then, there is still more that can be done. The fact though is that mothers have played indispensable roles in moulding the characters and lives of their children and helping them to become pillars in society.

As we saw in Chapter 5, it was DO's mother's strength of character and her determination to see her son receive education that ensured that he was able to continue with his schooling. If it had not been for his mother, DO's schooling would have been truncated very early and he would have ended up as an illiterate farmer. Needless to say, this book would never have been written and you would not be reading about all the interesting encounters and events narrated here.

Let every young girl, woman, mother and grandmother know that there is a divine role and destiny call they have to fulfil. They dare not fail.

In my book, *They Touched us for Good*, I wrote, among other things, about the overarching and continuing influence of a number of women and mothers. The story of my own mother and her enduring legacy is told in that book. The lives of the women (and men) recounted touched many people for good and changed destinies.

Let me mention only one here. She is Susanna Wesley, mother of the famous John Wesley and Charles Wesley. Her abiding life principle was, "I am content to fill a little space if God be glorified."

This is what I wrote in *They Touched us for Good*:

"Susanna was born almost 350 years ago and lived for 73 years. She bore 19 (yes, 19) children, 9 of whom died before adulthood. (Note the similarity with Awo Akua Dwiraa who had 15 children with 10 survived to adulthood.)

Needless to say she had no refrigerator, deep freezer, electric iron or any of the countless devices we now take for granted in our homes. Yet she ran her home very effectively and taught each of her children Latin and Greek. It is recorded that one son, John, was teaching Greek at Oxford by the age of 21. She ran a home school for all her children.

Her sons' John and Charles were powerhouses for the glory of the Lord. John Wesley preached to nearly a million people in his day. At the age of 70 he delivered the gospel message of salvation to 32,000 people— without the use of a microphone! He brought revival everywhere he travelled!

His brother Charles wrote over 9,000 hymns, many of which we still sing today. Hidden behind the door of our homes, we want our children to find a mum who prays diligently— no matter how busy or how hard the circumstances.

Now, back to Susanna Wesley. Dr John Edmund Haggai asks a question which he then proceeds to answer. The question: Did Susanna Wesley influence the world? The answer: Yes. Through her son John, she contributed to these tremendous accomplishments, among others: . . . the abolition of the slave trade . . . the launching of the industrial revolution . . . the establishment of the YMCA and YWCA . . . the multiplication of public libraries . . . the creation of the Salvation Army . . . the creation of orphanages . . . the founding of the Methodist Church and all the great institutions born out of the Methodist Church worldwide.

In Ghana, as in many parts of the world, the influence of the Methodist Church has been immense. Pause to ask yourself: where would we be without the contribution of the Methodist Church? Imagine that Wesley College, Wesley Girls High School and Mfantsipim School had not been established? Certainly an unimaginable vacuum would have been created. I am not a Methodist, but I know about the work that the Susanna Wesley Mission Auxiliary (SUWMA) is doing in many parts of Ghana. The list could go on and on.

Susanna was said to be a time-management genius. In addition to the formidable list of household chores and other assignments she had to attend to, she made sure that she set aside one hour each week to pray for each of her children. This was a woman who had her eyes on the future, and who was sure in her conviction that the seeds she was sowing and watering would yield manifold harvests in years to come. Ask yourself, what legacy are you leaving? Who is going to remember you 10 or 20 or 30 years after you are gone? If they do remember you, how are they going to remember you? I hear that the epitaph on the tomb of Susanna Wesley reads: "The gnawing tooth of time will ultimately reduce this marble memorial to dust, but the influence of this devout mother will live as long as time lasts". What a testimony! How amazing! How inspiring!"

I would also want you to come along with me to look at some women (mostly mothers) who displayed exceptional qualities in the life of Moses, described as the "friend of God" in the Bible. The circumstances surrounding the birth of Moses as recorded in the book of Exodus in the Bible have all the features of a modern day thriller.

Moses was born at a time when, due to the rising numbers of the Israelites who were in captivity in Egypt, Pharaoh, King of Egypt, feared that a time would come when the Israelites would outnumber the Egyptians and pose a security threat. He therefore decreed that the midwives in Egypt should kill all Hebrew (Israelite) baby boys at the point of their delivery. Obviously, he wanted the girls to be kept alive so that Egyptian men would marry them when they came of age.

The Hebrew (Israelite) midwives in charge of deliveries refused to carry out the order. Two of them are mentioned specifically in the account. They are Shifrah (Beautiful One) and Pu'ah (Girl). When they were found out and summoned before Pharaoh, they displayed great wisdom in their answers. Though not specifically stated, I want to believe that these two were mothers.

The next woman (and mother) I want to mention is Moses' mother. When the baby Moses, who had been saved from being killed at birth, was three months old and could no longer be hidden from the eagle eyes of Pharaoh's scouts on the lookout for Hebrew baby boys to kill, this devoted mother devised a scheme to try to save her boy. She put Baby Moses in a basket, took him to the river and stood a distance away to see what would happen.

The next woman is the daughter of Pharaoh who arrived at the river side and saw the baby in his basket floating on the water. Her heart went out to the baby and she ended up saving the boy and adopting him as her own son. The rest, as the saying goes, is history. There isn't time to provide the details of this fascinating story here. You can read them in the book of Exodus in the Old Testament of the Bible.

The Princess was tough and wise. She was also compassionate. She was not interested in destroying life, but rather in preserving it. She therefore used her position as Princess to nurture the baby Moses.

The common thread running through the examples of Susanna Wesley and the others mentioned here is the world view of these women. These epitomise the optimal development role and the characteristics a woman and a mother should play and exhibit. Wisdom, courage, fearlessness, assertiveness, confidence, single-mindedness and altruism. These and many more, are the characteristics displayed by all these women and mothers. I am pleased to say that DO's mother, Awo Akua Dwiraa, possessed some of these qualities. These characteristics of hers enabled her to have a vision of her son as an educated and useful member of society who would one day influence other lives for good if he was given the right foundations. This vision motivated her to stand her ground in getting DO's father to release the boy from the village and farm duties to resume schooling.

Let me repeat for emphasis that this book would not have been written if Awo Akua Dwiraa had not taken that decisive stand which changed the destiny of DO. She was, in the true sense, the one who helped DO to Cross the Bar.

Mothers, know that you have a crucial and irreplaceable role to play in the lives of your children and wards. Rise up to that responsibility. Posterity will be witness to the outcome of your efforts and praise you.

CHAPTER 19

Lessons from the Life of D. O. Amoafo

To have been blessed with long life as DO has, and to live to 90 years and still counting, is a blessing from God that most people do not experience. God blesses us in order that we may in turn be a blessing to others.

DO has never failed in admitting that he does not deserve so much grace. In his tribute to his late wife he was sad that she had rather gone ahead of him, because so far as he was concerned, she should have lived more years to enjoy more of her labour and toils. He has not minced words in confessing to his youthful exuberances and its consequences. To live to 90 and counting was just by the abundant Grace of God.

He, DO, has allowed this book to be written about him for us to have an in-depth look into his life and family history, just so that we may pick some lessons and best practices to help improve on ourselves and society; especially our families which are the basic units of the nation. He is worried that a lot of things have gone wrong. These are evident on our spiritual side, where there is a lot of corruption and deceit, and on the physical side, through the environmental pollution and filth we see around us. Additionally, our inter-personal relationships are poor, with a lot of envy, hatred and wickedness.

He agrees that the current generation is faced with many difficulties, trials, hardships and sometimes overwhelming obstacles. They need to hear the stories of those who have "crossed the bar" in spite of all the odds. They need to learn from such. At the end of the day, there is really nothing new under the sun. The circumstances, settings, players and dynamics may differ, but the principles to apply for effective living remain the same.

Based on the above statements, let's end this narration with ten lessons from the life of Daniel Opong Amoafo (DO). Let the reader pay attention to these lessons and apply them with other relevant ones for crossing the bars of life.

1. Whatever your hand finds to do, do it well.

2. Tomorrow does not belong to you. Do what you have to do now. Stop procrastination.

3. Never give up. Your persistence will yield a good harvest.

4. Nothing ventured, nothing gained.

5. Do what you can with what you have. He did what he could with what he had. He did not waste time longing for what others had.

6. Don't be afraid to seek help when in difficulty. He did this with his studies and the help he got yielded good results for him.

7. Hard work does not kill. On the contrary, it leads to prosperity.

8. There is no end to what you can achieve and become if you utilise your God-given talents well.

9. Genuine love, for instance the type shown him by his elder brothers Paul and J. A. Amoafo (who became his mentors), will always result in good and lasting generational impact.

10. Take good care of your children. They have been entrusted to you by God. Support them with all your resources and provide them with direction towards the right principles, standards and goals. They will turn out well and be a blessing to you and society.

APPENDIX 1

Tribute in Memory of
My Dear Wife and Confidante:
Mrs Margaret Boatemaa Amoafo

By Mr D.O. Amoafo

Adwoa, or Maggie, is how I always addressed my wife, and she would respond either with, Kwadwo or DO, depending on the mood or the reason for my calling her. We were together on this life's journey since 1954 when we first met. We eventually got married thanks to the blessing of our parents, Opanyin Kwaku Amoafo and Opanyin Kwabena Diawuo.

We came a long way, and weathered the storms together. But through all the changing scenes of life– in danger, darkness and troubles, Maggie was a pillar and a blessing to me and other members of my extended family such that words cannot adequately describe. As the only child of her mother, (whom I used to call 'Menua', and who would respond with the same Menua), we were bonded in this business of ... 'for better, for worse' and today I find myself at the,'...till death do us part, the final part of the solemn vow. Yet, I find it extremely difficult to comprehend or let go, for in my human self, I thought she would rather pay tribute to me and not the other way round because of the differences in our age and also for the fact that I have had more health challenges in recent times. But since November, 2017 when we both suffered the tragedy of losing Kwadwo, Maggie nurtured the pain of this loss, and it was difficult to get her back to her normal self.

Inspite of all that, I was sure I would pre-decease her and that she would live many more years and see to our grandchildren and even the great grandchildren before possibly joining us at the other side. But today I am devastated at the turn of events and this is to say the least.

Many of you gathered here or reading this piece know our story through her biography, and even personal experiences you have had with us, for we shared common friends and it will be useless or boring to repeat it. Instead, may I plead with you to rather allow me to use this occasion to say a very big thank you to my dear wife whose mortal remains is before us: for all the love, care and support she gave me as well as her tolerance and all that she had to endure during these 60 plus years we were together as man and wife. I was the naughty one, I was the trouble maker, I have been all that it takes to get any woman at her wits end. But with all these character traits and their accompanying troubles, Maggie remained resolute, and a strong pillar in the relationship.

In extreme difficulties and through the challenges of life, she always provided the solutions, and all my family members – from my deceased parents, through to my siblings, going down to my nephews and nieces and even great grand-children – have had good experiences with her. Through her generosity and open armed character, she brought them up to make them responsible members of the society. I thank her sincerely for nurturing our children and financially supporting their education and other critical needs. I thank her for being the woman of virtue, prayerful, with a good character wherever we trekked and also in our neighbourhood. Adwoa I am grateful.

It will be an understatement to say that my whole life is disoriented without you. There is no need to say how devastated I am by your sudden departure. It is difficult for me to keep going on in our home and seeing your regular sitting area empty. It will be hypocritical for me to say that it is well, but at the same time, I do not know where to direct my questions or who will provide a good answer to them than to turn to my BIBLE. Or to turn to God. For as with Job, the Lord gave and the Lord has taken away, Glory be to His Name.

Adwoa Boatemaa Akuamoah da yiye
Meda wo ase ahenewa

APPENDIX 2

One of the Saddest Periods of His Life.
When His Son Kwadwo Amoafo Died.

Tribute by Parents

We take consolation in the word of God as provided in Eccl 3:10-15.

'I know the heavy burdens that God has laid on us. He has set the right time for everything. He has given us a desire to know the future, but never gives us the satisfaction of fully understanding what he does. So I realise that all we can do is to be happy and do the best we can while we are still alive. All of us should eat and drink and enjoy what we have worked for. It is God's gift. I know that everything that God does will last forever. You can't add anything to it or take anything away from it. And one thing that God does is to make us stand in awe of him. Whatever happens or can happen has already happened before. God makes the same thing happen again and again.' Amen

"Kwadwo was born on the 22nd of September, 1958, 40 days after the death of his paternal grandfather, Opanyin Kwaku Amoafo. He was therefore named after him and christened Comforter at baptism.

His birth brought considerable COMFORT to the pain and grief his father (Mr. D. O. Amoafo) suffered at the loss of his dear father - Opanyin Kwaku Amoafo.

Looking back on his life, and what by the Grace of God he had accomplished in this rather short life; that is, the many souls he touched, and the relief he brought to many people who came into his life, we believe the name Comforter, given to him was very appropriate. His catch phrase was "mma biribiara nha wo," to wit, be not troubled.

He was such a joy to watch growing up directly after Kofi his senior brother. There was less than two years separating them and they were thus more or less like twins. However, they had very contrasting characters and this added so much fun to their infant days and activities. As parents, we did all that we could to bring all the siblings up in our Christian faith and belief. We tried to give them the best in education and nurture their social life such that our home was always full of children from other families and our close relations. This surely provided a congenial atmosphere culturally and a bigger network for them and helped in moulding their personality and character positively.

We cannot in this tribute recount the overwhelming support, love and care we have enjoyed from our children especially Kwadwo who lived with us all these years in Ghana and the pain is sharper if one considers that he was called to rest on that Sunday while in the process of doing another such service. His citation to his mother which he never had the opportunity to present at the glamorous function he was preparing to honour us speaks volumes of how he appreciated us. In return for his dedicated service we would have loved to present him with a beautiful citation on his 60th birthday which, we were looking forward to, but as it is; in the wisdom of God and our maker; today we pay this tribute to our dear son, we will surely miss him. Maggie his mother has this to say...

I felt a touch on my shoulders and that was Kwadwo waking me up: 'Maame medi wo koko no aba'. This became my morning routine as I underwent treatment and recovery at the 37th Military Hospital, in Accra for severe anaemia. On one such visit, I mentioned to Kwadwo in passing how uncomfortably hot the ward was. The next instant the ward was supplied with fans, not only for me, but for the comfort of all the others in the ward. Nothing different from the previous times I had been in hospitals for various ailments that plague my ailing body. This had been Kwadwo's attitude since childhood. On his way from school, he would pick the juiciest of fruits or the best of nuts as he and his friends walked home and bring them to me. He did not want to be with his grandmother who was supposed to babysit him for me so I could do other chores. He had to be with Maame. In his later years, he would pass through our home on his way out of Accra on his businesses to make sure we were in good shape or to find out if we wanted anything from his travels.

On his return to Accra, he would pass through our home to announce his return, set our minds at ease and bring all sorts of needed stuff to us before he continued to his abode. The no response to my phone calls that Sunday afternoon when I was anticipating his return set me wondering, but of course the news of his death which explained the silence to my calls has been extremely devastating.

Kwadwo you have lived a 100 years in my heart; you have been a dear son. You have been what your creator wanted you to be during the days of your life. In my humanity, I wish you had buried me, in my humanity I wish you were here, but the wisdom of God far surpasses the wisdom of humans and I know God's time is the best.

In Eccl. 3:1, it is written, *".... everything that happens in this world happens at the time God chooses"*. So I accept your call in good faith and as much as I wish you had lived to enjoy the fruits of your hard work, I know there is no joy on Earth that surpasses the joy in Heaven where *"there shall be no more night and they will not need light or sunlight because the Lord God will be their light and they will rule as kings for ever and ever"* (Rev. 22:5). God gave you to me and everyone else to enjoy for a period stipulated by Him. The time is up and He has taken you away from us humans. I will stay in my Christian faith and give thanks and glory to the Almighty for the gift of you… Kwadwo Amoafo the Comforter, for your awesome company and love over these years. I am going to miss you desperately, my son, but I know you are with the Lord our Maker, the end journey of all Christians. My dearest son, Kwadwo Amoafo, rest in perfect peace.

On my part as the father....

Kwadwo was the heaviest of all the seven children, a real Mummie's boy as indicated by his Mum's tribute. His support and protection dates back to infancy, I recall but for him I would have been long gone because once on our way from Dormaa Ahenkro (B/A) to Kumasi, we encountered a terrible road accident that would have ended our lives. At the time, Kwadwo, then only few months old was on my lap, and in my effort to protect him, I ducked under the front dashboard of the truck we were travelling in. This action saved me from the impact of the timber log from the truck our vehicle crashed into. That was the first service Kwadwo paid me as a son.

The second encounter was an experience I had during a trip to Dodowa to supervise a project. I became hypoglycaemic (low blood sugar level) and was in a state of confusion and disorientation; passers-by mistook me for a drunk. A God-sent 'Good Samaritan' got me to Dodowa Medical Facility and the staff members were able to contact Kwadwo through his details on my phone. I woke up to see him by my bedside where he had commandeered all the necessary resources to keep me alive.

On the morning of the Thursday before the weekend of this bitter, never to be forgotten experience, we were woken by the rattling of the main gate to the house. That was Kwadwo coming over to inspect the house with workmen to have it fully painted for his mother's birthday and the festive periods ahead. He and his siblings had carefully planned to honour us and especially their mother on her 80th birthday, to give her, her heart's desire which was to have the family house reconstructed.

Kwadwo lived up to his name as the Comforter and made us COMFORT-able.

APPENDIX 3

Amoafo Family Tree

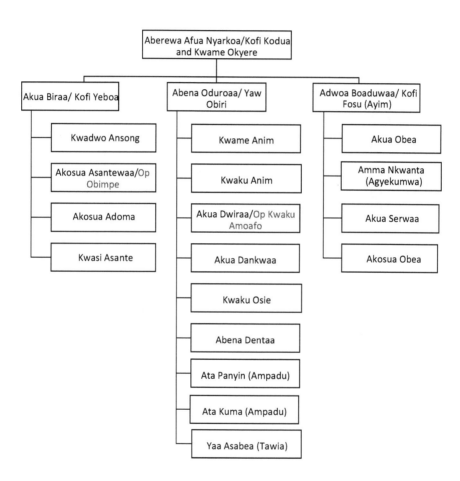

Index

ABOUT THE AUTHOR

Kofi Otutu Adu Labi is a lawyer, management consultant and author. He is also a Church Elder, teacher and preacher.

He was educated at Ofori Panin, Achimota School, University of Ghana and the University of Bradford School of Management. He also studied at Georgetown University Law Center, the International Law Institute (Washington DC), the Cranfield School of Management and London Business School. He is an alumnus of the Haggai Institute for Advanced Leadership, Hawaii.

He served as Adviser under two Governors of the Bank of Ghana (Dr Paul Acquah and Mr Kwesi Amissah-Arthur).

He started his banking career at the then SSB Bank (now Societé Generale Ghana) as a pioneering staff in 1976 and was the founding head of the Legal Department, before rising to the position of General Manager.

He has held a number of directorships including Commissioner, Securities and Exchange Commission Ghana, the National Pensions Regulatory Authority, Taysec Construction, Taysec Properties, Scripture Union Ghana, Victory Presbyterian Church School and the Bible Society of Ghana. He is a Trustee of the Presbyterian Church of Ghana Education Foundation as well as a Member of Council of the Christian Service

University College, Kumasi. He is a Trustee of the Esther Ocloo Memorial Foundation. He has served as Senior Presbyter and Presbyter at the Dansoman Emmanuel and Victory (Fafraha) congregations of the Presbyterian Church of Ghana respectively.

He is a member of the Advisory Board of the Ghana Association of Writers (GAW). He has written eight other books of which five have so far been endorsed by the National Council for Curriculum and Assessment (NaCCA) as supplementary readers for schools in Ghana.

He is a recipient of the GAW Achievement Award, 2019.

He has been married to Elioenai since 1978 and they have five adult children and three grandchildren.

Made in the USA
Middletown, DE
20 October 2022

13171853R00106